ROBERT NIESE, PHD

BACKYARD
SCIENCE &
DISCOVERY
WORKBOOK

PACIFIC NORTHWEST

ADVENTURE PUBLICATIONS

TABLE OF CONTENTS

ABOUT THIS BOOK

What does it mean to be a naturalist? Naturalists are more than just overenthusiastic nature-nuts. We are observers—we explore, we discover, and we document. In the words of MythBusters' Adam Savage, "The only difference between messing around and science is writing it down." We keep journals, take notes, and accumulate our observations through time to gain a more complete understanding of the world and how it varies from place to place, season to season, and year to year.

But we are not only observers, we also must be educators. Naturalists are the quiet stewards of our public lands and wild places. We defend these habitats through education. By learning about rocks or birds or flowers, we are cultivating genuine connections to nature, which, hopefully, leads others to become stewards as well.

This is my goal with this workbook—to help young learners connect with the natural world and to practice being naturalists. This book encourages exploration, careful observation, and curiosity. And I hope that, by educating these young minds, they might become naturalists too.

This book features 25 hands-on science projects, such as raising caterpillars, making mushroom art, identifying animal tracks; 10 simple, fun introductions to the region's habitats, birds, seasons, and rocks and minerals, and more than a dozen independent inquiries to help you make hypotheses, observe nature, and practice your skills as a naturalist.

Every piece of the natural world is an exciting opportunity for discovery. Whether it's a rock, a bug, or a feather, connecting to nature inspires curiosity and discovery. These are the hallmarks of fun and genuine learning.

So get outside, flip over rocks, put leaves under the magnifying glass, collect cones—do it all and record and share your observations! That's what makes it science!

Robert Niese

GEOGRAPHY OF
THE PACIFIC NORTHWEST

Also known as Cascadia, the Pacific Northwest includes all of Washington, Oregon, and Idaho. Some naturalists consider parts of California, Montana, Canada, and even Alaska as part of the region as well. Practice your geography and label the states below.

Bonus points if you can name the state capitals of each one.

Answers on page 140!

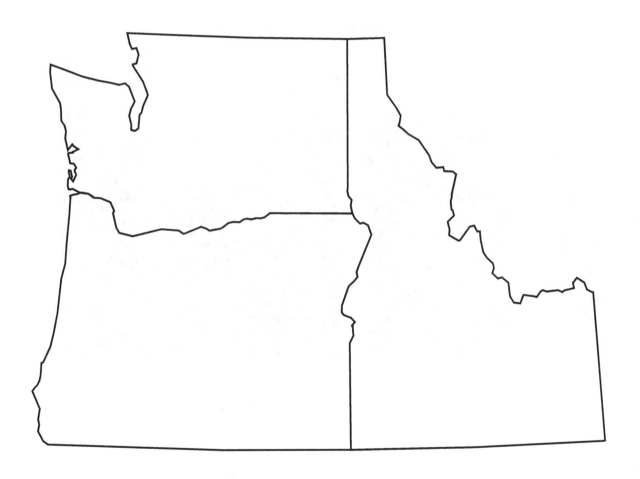

ID _____   WA _____

OR _____

GET TO KNOW THE PACIFIC NORTHWEST'S BIOMES

A **biome** is a community of animals and plants that live in a specific kind of climate and environment. The Pacific Northwest has some of the wettest and driest biomes in North America! Getting to know our region's biomes is a great way to learn more about your state and the habitats that exist in your very own backyard.

You've probably heard of some biomes before: deserts, rainforests, and so on.

The Pacific Northwest is home to three major biomes:

1. Coniferous Forests

2. Temperate Rainforests

3. Dry Shrublands and Deserts

QUICK QUIZ

Which biome do you live in? Use the map on the next page!

_____

_____

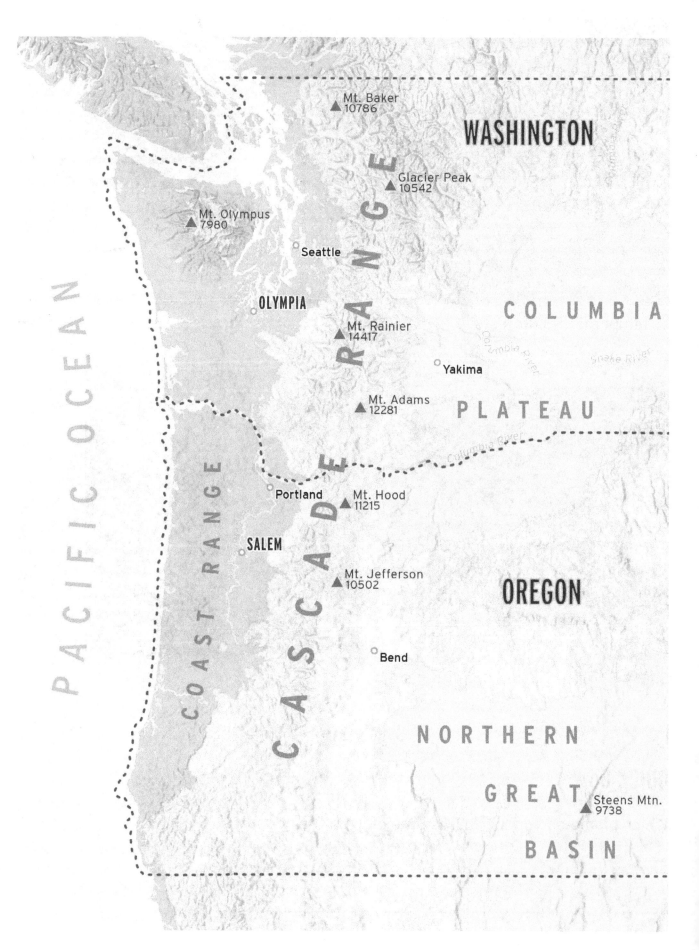

WASHINGTON

▲ Mt. Baker
10786

▲ Glacier Peak
10542

▲ Mt. Olympus
7980

Seattle

OLYMPIA

▲ Mt. Rainier
14417

COLUMBIA

○ Yakima

▲ Mt. Adams
12281

PLATEAU

PACIFIC OCEAN

COAST RANGE

C A S C A D E   R A N G E

Columbia River

Snake River

Columbia River

Portland

▲ Mt. Hood
11215

SALEM

OREGON

▲ Mt. Jefferson
10502

○ Bend

NORTHERN

GREAT

▲ Steens Mtn.
9738

BASIN

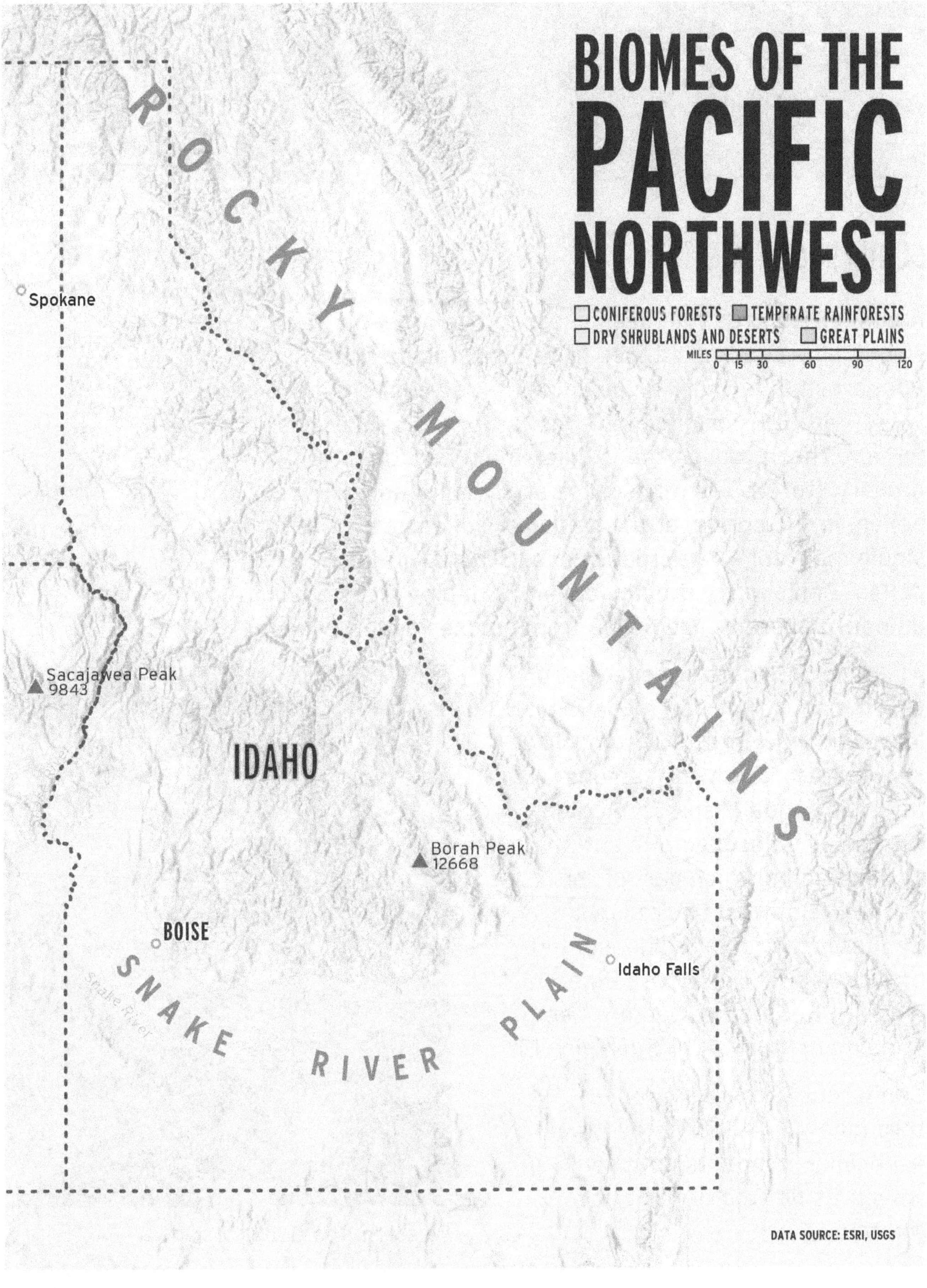

BIOMES OF THE
PACIFIC
NORTHWEST

□ CONIFEROUS FORESTS ■ TEMPERATE RAINFORESTS
□ DRY SHRUBLANDS AND DESERTS □ GREAT PLAINS

MILES | 0 15 30 60 90 120

DATA SOURCE: ESRI, USGS

Spokane

ROCKY MOUNTAINS

Sacajawea Peak
9843

IDAHO

Borah Peak
12668

BOISE

Idaho Falls

Snake River

SNAKE RIVER PLAIN

CONIFEROUS FORESTS

A **conifer** is a tree that has cones. You've probably seen woody pine cones like those from the Douglas-fir or Ponderosa Pine, but did you know that all conifers make two different kinds of cones? The large woody ones are female. They produce seeds (like pine nuts from the grocery store!). The male cones are smaller and produce pollen. In the spring, at the height of pollen season, a single male cone can produce over 30,000 grains of pollen! Don't worry though, pollen from pine trees doesn't influence allergies like pollen from grasses and ragweed.

Almost all conifers are **evergreen**, which means they don't lose their leaves in the winter. But some, like the Western Larch, are famous for their annual displays of color as their needles die off in autumn. Depending on which part of the Pacific Northwest you're in, Coniferous Forests are dominated by Douglas-fir, Ponderosa Pine, Western Red Cedar, Western Larch, Engelmann Spruce, or Subalpine Fir.

Western Red Cedar forest

Coniferous Forests are found throughout the Pacific Northwest, especially in mountainous regions where it's not too dry and not too rainy.

QUICK QUIZ

Which of the following trees is evergreen?

A. Western Larch B. Subalpine Fir C. Black Hawthorn D. Black Cottonwood

Answer on page 140!

1. Make a list of the evergreen trees near you.

_____

_____

_____

_____

2. What **deciduous** trees (trees that lose their leaves) are nearby?

_____

_____

_____

_____

MAKE A COLLECTION OF PACIFIC NORTHWEST CONES

Even if you don't live in the Coniferous Forest biome, you can still find conifers in most neighborhoods in the Pacific Northwest. Conifer cones come in all different shapes and sizes. Most have papery or woody scales. Some really weird ones, like the cones from junipers, are covered in hard bluish-purple flesh and look more like berries. Some trees that aren't conifers produce seed pods that look a bit like cones too. The Alder, for example, makes a cone-like structure called a catkin. Look for cones, catkins, and other seed pods on the ground around large trees. Try organizing your collection using a cardboard egg carton! Label each cone or seed pod by writing its name on the edge of each dimple. You can even use the lid to hold really big cones like those from Sugar Pines.

Alder catkin

Douglas-fir cone

Ponderosa Pine cone

Sugar Pine cone

TEMPERATE RAINFORESTS

I bet you've heard of rainforests before. But did you know that the Pacific Northwest is home to some of the only **temperate** rainforests in the world? The word temperate means mild or moderate and refers to the cooler climate zones between the tropics (around the **equator**) and the polar zones. Most rainforests exist in areas with a tropical climate, which is what makes our temperate rainforests so special!

As you might have guessed, Temperate Rainforests are very wet places. But not all their water comes from rain. In our southernmost rainforests, rain contributes around 70 inches of water each year, but fog contributes another 30 to 40 inches! As moist air from the Pacific Ocean moves onto land, it condenses and forms rain and fog—the lifeforce of all rainforests.

All that moisture means that plants in our temperate rainforests have to like it wet! Plants like mosses, ferns, and Oxalis wood sorrels blanket the forest floor, while Douglas-fir, Western Red Cedar, Sitka Spruce, and Western Hemlock dominate the canopy. In between, Big-leaf Maples, Red Alders, Pacific Madrone, and Pacific Rhododendron are common, and fungi sprout from every surface. These rich forests are home to nearly 300 species of birds and over 70 species of mammals.

MAKE A COLLECTION OF PRESSED LEAVES

Leaves can be pressed and dried to preserve their beauty or to turn into your very own art project.

- Start by collecting neat leaves, either fresh from trees in the summer or from the ground in the fall.

- Place your leaves between two sheets of heavy construction paper. Thick paper helps absorb moisture from the leaves as they dry.

- Now place your leaf sandwich between the pages of a big book. Then add some more big books on top of it, for good measure.

- Place your stack of leaf-filled books in a warm, dry place for four to ten days (depending on the leaf thickness).

That's it! You've now got a lovely preserved leaf! Leaves preserved by using this method should retain their color for many years. But be careful, they're brittle!

DRY SHRUBLANDS AND DESERTS

Between the Pacific Northwest's mountain ranges lay vast regions of deserts and dry shrublands. The Cascade Range acts like a barrier for clouds that are heavy with water, so by the time they reach the Columbia Plateau and Great Basin, they're as dry as a bone. Parts of Central Washington, Central and Southeastern Oregon, and Southern Idaho receive only 5 or 6 inches of precipitation (rain and snow, combined!) each year. But just because these habitats are dry, it doesn't mean they aren't bursting with life!

In areas where it's slightly wetter, Big Sagebrush dominates the landscape. This plant is a keystone species for our dry shrubland habitats, which are aptly called sagebrush steppe habitats. The Big Sagebrush provides shade for other plants to grow and shelter for animals that are **endemic** to the sagebrush steppe, such as the Greater Sage-Grouse, Brewer's Sparrow, Pygmy Rabbit, and Pronghorn.

Greater Sage-Grouse

DID YOU KNOW?

The sagebrush steppe is also home to one of the world's largest migratory events? Every summer, migrating bands of Mormon Crickets travel through the sagebrush steppe looking for food. Each swarm of flightless hungry insects can contain millions of individuals that can quickly devour crops. They also become a hazard for drivers because the endless supply of roadkilled insects can make highways dangerously slick with cricket guts. Gross!

Mormon Cricket

Thousands of Mormon Crickets crossing a road

QUICK QUESTION

In the sentence, "The Big Sagebrush provides shade for other plants to grow and shelter for animals that are endemic to the sagebrush steppe," what do you think the word endemic means?

A. Widespread and diseased

B. Native and restricted to a certain area

C. Finished and not continuing

D. Dedicated and committed to a cause

Answer on page 140!

THEN VS. NOW

GEOLOGIC HISTORY

The landscape of the Pacific Northwest has been shaped by catastrophic natural forces. The Columbia Plateau and Northern Great Basin were completely flooded with lava between 17 and 14 million years ago. The lava flowed and cooled repeatedly until, in some places, it became more than a mile thick! The resulting rock formations are called basalts, and they blanket an area of the Pacific Northwest that spans more than 81,000 square miles—that's larger than the entire state of Washington!

The Columbia River Basalts were formed by volcanic activity surrounding the Yellowstone Hotspot. But you might be wondering, how could the Yellowstone Hotspot, which is all the way over in Wyoming, cause the massive lava floods here in the Pacific Northwest? Well, because of the movement of Earth's tectonic plates, the Yellowstone Hotspot was actually beneath Oregon 17 million years ago. Over time, the North American tectonic plate has slowly

Mount St. Helens before and after it erupted in 1980.

moved to the southwest, and the land above the hotspot has suffered cataclysmic volcanic events as a result. The trail of destruction left behind by this movement created the Snake River Plain and some of Idaho's most famous geologic features, like the Craters of the Moon National Monument.

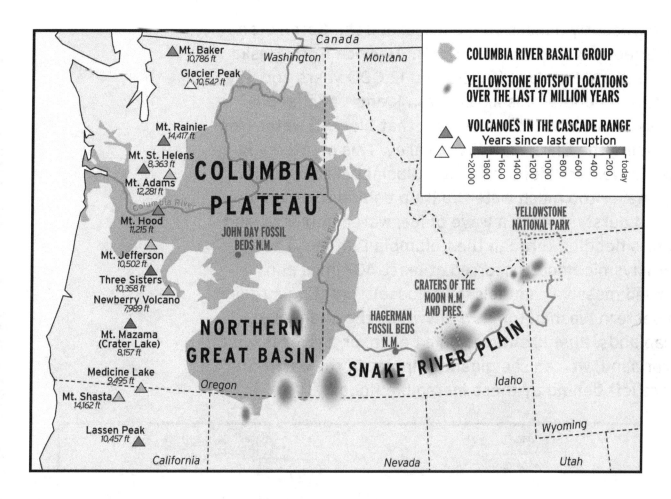

QUICK QUESTION

If you live in the valleys and foothills surrounding the Cascade Mountain Range, you're probably familiar with some of the Pacific Northwest's most prominent volcanoes. The Cascade Range is home to dozens of volcanoes, most of which have erupted at least once in the last 2,000 years. Which volcano is closest to where you live? When was the last time it erupted?

THEN VS. NOW

GEOLOGIC HISTORY

More recently a massive **glacier** called the Cordilleran Ice Sheet covered western North America from Alaska to Montana. Between 18,000 and 12,000 years ago, the southern edge of this ice sheet in Idaho's panhandle occasionally created an ice dam that blocked water from escaping the Clark Fork River Valley. This created a huge lake in western Montana called Glacial Lake Missoula. Whenever too much water built up behind the dam, it would burst, sending a wave of ice, water, boulders, and debris flooding through the Columbia Plateau. These cataclysmic floods occurred at least 40 times and **eroded** massive channels in the basalt, creating a region in eastern Washington now known as the channeled scablands. Just like waves on a beach, or a river flowing over sand, we can see gigantic ripples in the earth that were left behind by these incredible floods.

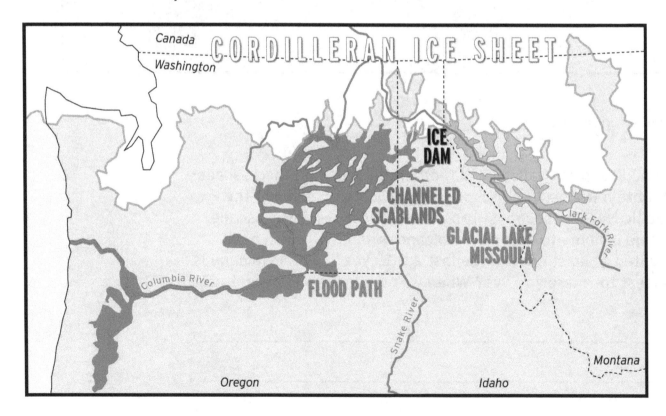

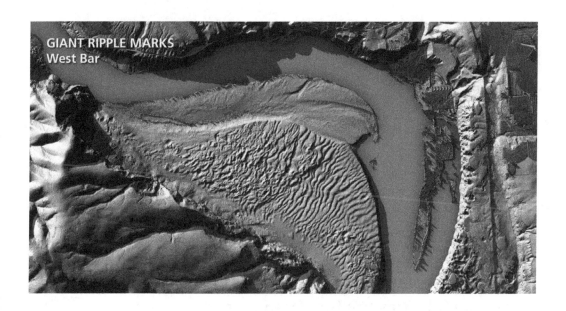

GIANT RIPPLE MARKS
West Bar

QUICK QUESTION

Even though the gigantic Cordilleran Ice Sheet is gone, there are still smaller glaciers in the Pacific Northwest. Where do you think you might be able to find some of the last of the Pacific Northwest's glaciers?

GLACIERS
Mount Rainier

THEN VS. NOW

HUMAN HISTORY

THE FIRST NATIVE AMERICANS

Humans first arrived in North America when they crossed an ancient land bridge that used to connect Alaska and Siberia. That makes the Pacific Northwest, including Alaska and British Columbia, the very first places to have human inhabitants on this continent. In Washington, Oregon, and Idaho, specifically, evidence indicates that humans have lived here for between 10,000 and 15,000 years. Along the Columbia River, some excellent fishing locations have been continuously inhabited for over 10,000 years—the longest of any location in North America.

Dipnet fishing for salmon at Kettle Falls today, in 1941, and in the 1800s.

THE FIRST EUROPEAN EXPLORERS

The west coast of the Americas was visited by a variety of Europeans, including the Spanish, British, Russians, and French. In 1804, after the French sold the land west of the Mississippi River to the United States (known as the Louisiana Purchase), the US ordered Meriwether Lewis and William Clark to lead an expedition to explore the Pacific Northwest. Their journey took them along the Clearwater, Snake, and Columbia Rivers, where many of their camps are designated historic sites today.

NATIVE AMERICANS IN THE PACIFIC NORTHWEST TODAY

After more than 10,000 years of human habitation, it's no wonder that the cultures, languages, and histories of modern Native peoples are so diverse. There are over 50 distinct languages spoken by modern Native peoples in the Pacific Northwest today and over 40 different sovereign nations (governments, tribes, and groups of tribes that are independent from the United States government) still present in Washington, Oregon, and Idaho.

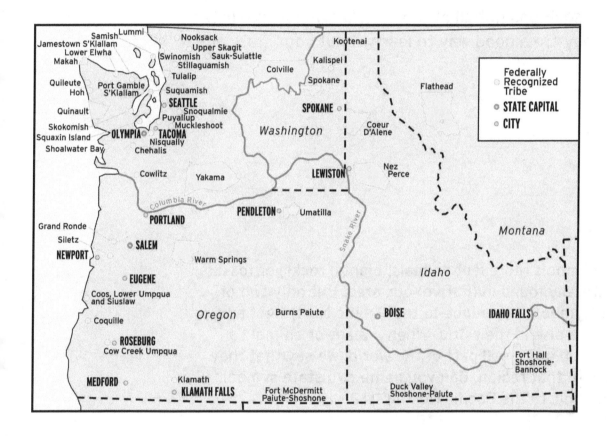

QUICK QUESTION

Wherever you live in the Pacific Northwest, the land around you was once inhabited by Native Americans, and many still continue their traditions and customs nearby. What tribes are in your area?

STATE SYMBOLS

Another good way to get to know the region is by learning your state's official symbols. From the state bird and flower, which you might know already, to lesser-known categories, such as state amphibian, gemstone, or **fossil**, these iconic plants, animals, and materials are usually selected because they have a long history with the state. Of course, not every state has symbols for the same categories—some states even have a state soil!—and not all of the state's symbols are listed here. Still, they are a good way to learn about your state and its wildlife.

QUICK QUIZ

Most state symbols represent animals, plants, rocks, or fossils that are naturally found in (**native**) our area. But only two of these state symbols are unique to the Pacific Northwest and found nowhere else in the world. When a plant or animal can only be found in one small part of the world, we say that they are endemic to that region. Can you name two state symbols that are endemic to the Pacific Northwest?

1._____   2._____

Answers on page 140!

WASHINGTON

Willow Goldfinch

Bird

Pacific Rhododendron

Flower

Petrified Wood

Gem

Western Hemlock

Tree

Pacific Chorus Frog

Amphibian

Olympic Marmot

Endemic Mammal

Orca

Marine Mammal

Steelhead Trout

Fish

Apple

Fruit

Green Darner Dragonfly

Insect

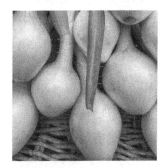

Walla Walla Sweet Onion

Vegetable

Columbian Mammoth

Fossil

STATE SYMBOLS

OREGON

Western Meadowlark

Bird

Oregon Grape

Flower

Oregon Sunstone

Gemstone

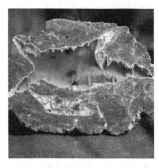

Thunderegg

Rock

Dawn Redwood

Fossil

Douglas-fir

Tree

Chinook Salmon

Fish

American Beaver

Animal

Oregon Swallowtail Butterfly

Insect

Brewer's Yeast

Microbe

Pacific Golden Chanterelle

Mushroom

IDAHO

Mountain Bluebird

Bird

Syringa (Mock Orange)

Flower

Idaho Giant Salamander

Amphibian

Hagerman Horse

Fossil

Cutthroat Trout

Fish

Huckleberry

Fruit

Star Garnet

Gem

Appaloosa

Horse

Monarch Butterfly

Insect

Western White Pine

Tree

Potato

Vegetable

GET TO KNOW THE SEASONS & THE WEATHER

The seasons of the year are like the hours on a clock: winter is the night, spring is the morning, summer is the afternoon, and fall is twilight. If you pay attention to this seasonal clock, and the animals and plants found during each season, you'll be studying **phenology**. Phenology is the study of the cycles of the seasons and the natural world over time. By studying the phenology of your area—when certain birds arrive in spring, or when huckleberries are first ripe in summer, or when the first frost comes—you'll learn a lot about the natural world around you and what to expect next.

IT DEPENDS ON WHERE YOU LIVE

Phenology is very different across the Pacific Northwest. The Pacific Ocean prevents coastal areas from ever getting too hot or too cold and creates a lot of clouds. The Cascade Mountains are like a giant barrier preventing those clouds and their moisture from reaching the eastern parts of Oregon, Washington, and Idaho. This means that weather and temperatures can be very different on a single day, depending on whether you are on the west or east side of the Cascades. For example, in the last week of October in 2019, the coastal city of Brookings, Oregon, experienced several days above 70°F (up to 86°F) while Pocatello, Idaho, experienced its coldest October ever (with a record low of -6°F!).

LET'S STUDY PHENOLOGY!

START OUT BY MAKING SOME PREDICTIONS

Before you start observing, see what you already know. Make some predictions about when you expect to see the wildlife around you. You might not have seen all of these animals or plants before. If not, that's OK, but make predictions about those you recognize.

LEARN A NEW TERM: F.O.T.Y.

Birders are famous for making many careful observations about when and where they see certain species of birds. Many birders keep F.O.T.Y. records noting the **First Of The Year** sighting for migratory species. Try keeping your own F.O.T.Y. records for your favorite migratory birds! Or explore the F.O.T.Y. sightings on eBird for your county by visiting eBird.org/explore. Search for your county, change the time period from "All Years" to "Current Year," and then select "First Seen."

LET'S MAKE SOME OBSERVATIONS!

When we study phenology, we keep records of what times of the year certain plants and animals are seen doing certain things. When does a flower bloom? When do leaves change color? When do sparrows lay their eggs? Some naturalists keep a small notepad with them to write down certain events. Some gardeners take detailed notes and compare their gardens to what is available at farmer's markets. But anyone can take a picture with a smartphone to create a record of the exact date and time of flowers blooming, etc.

Bohemian Waxwing migration

GET TO KNOW THE SEASONS & THE WEATHER

To get you thinking about phenology, try making observations to answer the following questions throughout the year:

In which season do you notice hummingbirds the most?

_____

In which month?

_____

In which month do cherry trees bloom where you live?

_____

In which month do buttercups bloom where you live?

_____

In which months do the maple trees get their leaves where you live?

_____

When do they lose them?

_____

In which month do larches start growing new needles where you live?

_____

When do they turn yellow?

_____

Rufous
Hummingbird

Buttercups

Cherry blossoms

Indian Plum

When are huckleberries ripe where you live?

_____

When do you start to see fresh chanterelles or morels at your local farmer's market?

_____

In which month(s) do you see the most dragonflies?

_____

Do you have apple or pear trees nearby?

_____

In which season can you harvest apples or pears?

_____

Does it normally snow where you live?

_____

Does it snow more or less than the national average (28")?

_____

Huckleberry

Cardinal Meadowhawk

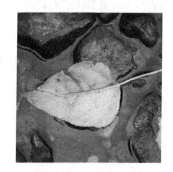

Cottonwood leaf

Snowflakes

DID YOU KNOW?

That some parts of the Pacific Northwest rarely get snow? The average for the whole country is 28 inches of snow per year. How does your area compare to this yearly average? Is it higher or lower where you live? Visit Weather-US.com, find your city, and choose "Climate" to view your average snowfall.

DO-IT-YOURSELF PHENOLOGY

The easiest way to start studying phenology is to observe one type of plant or animal throughout the year. Try this with the plants or animals in your yard. For example, if you have a cottonwood or another flowering tree nearby, keep track of when it loses it leaves, and then, in the spring, when the buds emerge, flowers and leaves form, and when fruit (or seed pods) develops. Jot down a few notes about the weather over the past few days, too, as rain and temperature are two of the drivers of natural phenomena.

For example, you might want to keep track of things like:

Year: _____

Buds form: _____

Flowers form: _____

Leaves emerge: _____

Seeds form: _____

Tree is fully "leafed out": _____

Leaves change colors in fall: _____

Leaves start falling off tree: _____

Then, keep track of that same tree, and see how different those same dates are. Does the tree have buds the same day of each year? How about seeds? What was the weather like? Notice how different types of trees have differing patterns of phenology. Do flowers or leaves appear first? Does the flowering period happen all at once, or is it stretched out over a couple months? How do those plants compare to the ones that kept their leaves all year?

Year: _____

Buds form: _____

Flowers form: _____

Leaves emerge: _____

Seeds form:_____

Tree is fully "leafed out":_____

Leaves change colors in fall:_____

Leaves start falling off tree: _____

Cottonwood leaves in summer

Cottonwood leaves in fall

PHENOLOGY CALENDAR:
SPRING

Use the phenology calendars on the following pages to help you as you make observations. Remember, the exact timing of these events varies by year, elevation, and by location throughout the Pacific Northwest.

Sage Buttercup

FEBRUARY TO MARCH: THE FIRST SIGNS OF SPRING

- Indian Plum begins to leaf-out and bloom in the west
- Willows are some of the first shrubs to bloom
- Sage Buttercup blooms in the east
- Salmonberry produces big green buds
- Tens of thousands of Snow Geese migrate through the Lower Klamath National Wildlife Refuge
- Tree Swallows arrive
- Mountain Bluebirds arrive in the east

Tree Swallow

What I spotted:

_____

_____

_____

_____

_____

_____

_____

Mountain Bluebird

MARCH TO APRIL: SPRING ARRIVES!

- Larches begin to grow needles
- Skunk cabbage blooms
- Bigleaf Maple is in full bloom in the west (attracting warblers)
- Most warblers arrive
- Salmonberry is in full bloom in the west (attracting Rufous Hummingbirds)
- Rufous Hummingbirds arrive
- Western Meadowlarks begin singing
- Chinook Salmon begin their spring runs
- Thousands of Sandhill Cranes migrate north
- Mourning Cloak Butterflies begin defending territory
- Bumblebees begin flying regularly

What I spotted:

_____

_____

_____

_____

_____

_____

_____

_____

_____

Western Larch

Bigleaf Maple

Salmonberry

Mourning Cloak Butterfly

APRIL TO MAY: SPRING IS IN FULL SWING

- Serviceberry (Saskatoon) is in full bloom
- Balsamroot begins to bloom in the east
- Lupines begin to bloom in the east
- Ponderosa Pines' pollen production peaks
- Pacific Wrens begin singing regularly
- The first Vaux's Swifts arrive
- The first Western Tanagers arrive
- The first Bullock's Orioles arrive
- Hundreds of thousands of shorebirds migrate through Grays Harbor
- Morel hunting season begins
- Migratory bats arrive
- Black Bears emerge from their dens

What I spotted:

_____

_____

_____

_____

_____

_____

_____

_____

_____

Ponderosa Pine pollen

Pacific Wren

Western Tanager

Balsamroot and lupine

PHENOLOGY CALENDAR: SUMMER

MAY TO JUNE: THE FIRST SIGNS OF SUMMER

- Cottonwoods release their fluffy seeds
- Syringa (Mock Orange) blooms
- Chokecherries bloom
- Nootka Roses bloom
- Bitterroot blooms
- Salmonberries ripen
- Bighorn Sheep lambs are born
- Pronghorn fawns are born

What I spotted:

_____

_____

_____

_____

_____

_____

_____

_____

_____

Pronghorn
with fawn

Cottonwood

Nootka Rose

JUNE TO JULY: IT'S SUMMERTIME!

- Oregon Swallowtails are active
- Dragonfly adults emerge, and you can sometimes see dozens at a time
- Ten-lined June Beetles start appearing at porch lights
- Common Nighthawks call and display in the evenings
- Townsend's Big-eared Bats (and most other species) give birth to their pups
- Camas bulbs are harvested
- Walla Walla onion season begins
- Historically, salmon runs on the Columbia River peaked

Ten-lined June Beetle

JULY TO AUGUST: SUMMER BEGINS TO FADE

- Mountain meadows finally bloom
- Yellow Pond Lily blooms (but in warmer water in the western lowlands, this can occur as early as May!)
- Thousands of Western Toadlets (young adult toads) migrate from ponds into the forest
- Chokecherries ripen
- Huckleberry season peaks in the east
- Sockeye Salmon runs occur around Puget Sound

Common Nighthawk

What I spotted:

_____

_____

_____

_____

_____

_____

Yellow Pond Lily

Chokecherries

PHENOLOGY CALENDAR:
FALL

AUGUST TO SEPTEMBER: THE FIRST SIGNS OF FALL

- Ninebark leaves begin to turn red
- Huckleberry bushes begin to turn red
- Thimbleberry leaves begin to turn yellow
- Boletes, chanterelles, and other fall fungi become abundant
- Apple and pear Harvest begins

What I spotted:

_____

_____

_____

_____

_____

_____

_____

_____

_____

_____

Ninebark leaves

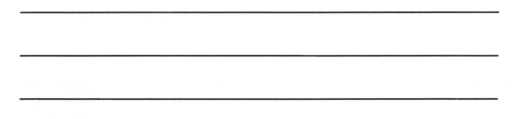

Thimbleberry

Late-summer mushroom

SEPTEMBER TO OCTOBER: AUTUMN ARRIVES!

- Quaking Aspen and cottonwoods turn yellow
- Willows turn yellow
- Vine Maples turn red
- Larches begin to turn golden
- Garry Oak acorns begin to fall
- Elk bugle and rut
- Chanterelle hunting season peaks in wet forests
- Salmon spawning season begins
- Mountain Bluebirds begin migrating south
- Polyphemus moths pupate (overwinter as pupa)
- Gray Whales begin their migration south
- Hazelnut harvest peaks
- Idaho russet potatoes are harvested

OCTOBER TO NOVEMBER: THE FINAL DAYS OF FALL

- Evergreen Huckleberry harvest peaks (in the west)
- Thousands of Sandhill Cranes migrate south
- Coho and Chum Salmon spawn in neighborhoods around Puget Sound
- Black Bears head into their winter dens for hibernation
- When the first snowfall occurs in the east (a good time to start looking for animal tracks!)
- Average date of first frost in the west

What I spotted:

_____

_____

_____

_____

_____

Quaking Aspen

Elk

Sandhill Crane

Chum Salmon

PHENOLOGY CALENDAR: WINTER

NOVEMBER TO DECEMBER

- Rain falls most regularly in the west
- Bighorn Sheep rut begins
- Thousands of Snow Geese migrate south through the Skagit Wildlife Area
- Rare Gyrfalcons and Snowy Owls appear near wetlands to hunt waterfowl

Bighorn Sheep

DECEMBER TO JANUARY

- Short-eared Owls patrol open fields and wetlands
- Snow falls most regularly in the east

JANUARY TO FEBRUARY

- Bald Eagles congregate in large numbers at wetlands
- Black Bear cubs are born

What I spotted in the winter:

_____

_____

_____

_____

_____

_____

Short-eared Owl

Bald Eagle

YOUR STATE'S MAJOR FARM CROPS & FARM PRODUCTS

The Pacific Northwest's rich volcanic history has created some very fertile areas. Much of the country's orchard crops are produced here and Washington leads the world in hops production—a small, fragrant cone-like flower used in brewing beer. Below are the top crops or **commodities** (agricultural products) in the Pacific Northwest.

IDAHO

- **Potatoes**
  Idaho grows more than 30 varieties of potatoes and produces nearly ⅓ of all the potatoes in the US.

- **Wheat**
  Wheat is the second-biggest agricultural product in Idaho

- **Hay**
  Idaho produces more organic hay than any other state and is the second-largest producer of alfalfa hay in the US

- **Mint**
  Idaho is the third-largest producer of mint in the US

- **Dairy**
  Idaho is the third-largest producer of cheese in the US

OREGON

- **Hazelnuts**
  Oregon is the largest producer of hazelnuts in the US and the fourth-largest in the world

- **Dungeness Crab**
  Oregon is the number-one producer of Dungeness Crabs in the US

- **Christmas Trees**
  Oregon produces more Christmas trees than any other state

- **Pears**
  Oregon is the second-largest producer of pears in the US

- **Blueberries**
  Oregon is the second-largest producer of blueberries in the US

- **Cranberries**
  Oregon is the third-largest producer of cranberries in the US

WASHINGTON

- **Raspberries**
  Over 90 percent of the nation's frozen red raspberries produced in the US are grown in Washington

- **Apples**
  Washington is the largest producer of apples in the US

- **Cherries**
  Washington is the largest producer of cherries in the US

- **Pears**
  Washington is the largest producer of pears in the US

- **Hops**
  Washington is the largest producer of hops in the world

- **Potatoes**
  Washington is the number-two producer of potatoes in the US

- **Onions**
  Nearly a quarter of all onions in the US are grown in Washington, making it the second-largest producer

Idaho potatoes

Oregon hazelnuts

Washington raspberries

QUICK QUIZ

You might have noticed that many state symbols are also important agricultural products. There are two missing, though! What delicious state symbols are not on this list? Do you know why?

_____

_____

Answers on page 140!

ASSEMBLING A COLLECTION OF MINERALS & GEMS

The Pacific Northwest is rich with interesting gems and minerals. In fact, Idaho's state nickname is the Gem State, and Central Oregon is known as the Rockhounding Capital of the World! There are lots of interesting rocks to hunt for in our area! Some of the most unique are honored as state symbols and can be found in very few other countries. Because so many people love to find and collect these gems, minerals, and fossils, there are many sites on public lands where rockhounding is encouraged! Take advantage of these cool locations to build your own collection!

Rules for Rockhounding: Rockhounding rules are different in each state, so be sure you look up information on your state's regulatory agency (links below). In general, you are allowed to collect rocks, gems, and fossils for fun or education on all public lands except national parks, national monuments, national wildlife refuges, national scenic areas, and tribal lands.
You are also typically not allowed to collect archaeological or historic artifacts, meteorites, or vertebrate fossils. In some locations there is a weight limit on how much you can take (there are usually signs posted with this information). There are also sometimes special rules for gold panning, specifically. When in doubt, check for information and notices posted at the entrance to the parking area or trailhead. Remember, do not collect on private property unless you have permission from the landowners.

Learn more about rockhounding in your state:

OREGON   Department of Geology and Mineral Industries
(Oregon.gov/DOGAMI)

WASHINGTON   Department of Natural Resources
(dnr.wa.gov/rockhounding)

IDAHO   Department of Lands
(www.idl.idaho.gov/mining-minerals/rockhounding/)

What you'll find: The most common gems and minerals in the Pacific Northwest are agates, jasper, geodes and thundereggs, opal, petrified wood, agatized wood (limb casts), and obsidian. There are hundreds of locations where you can find these neat rocks, and the State Departments (previous page) have maps with detailed directions on where to hunt for each. Here's a bit of information about these common gems, minerals, and fossils.

QUICK DEFINITION

A **mineral** usually consists of a combination of chemical elements. For example, table salt is a mineral (also known as halite) made of two elements, sodium and chlorine. Sometimes, a single **chemical element** (like gold or silver) can be found in nature; those are considered minerals too. A **rock** is a combination of at least two minerals.

Rocky beach near La Push, Washington

Fossil shells near Silverton, Oregon

ASSEMBLING A COLLECTION OF MINERALS & GEMS

AGATE

A variety of **chalcedony** (a type of quartz with very small crystals) that is **translucent** (allows some light to pass through it) and extremely variable. Rockhounding sites throughout the Pacific Northwest will each have their own types of common agates. Some of the most valued are those with swirled grains and distinctive layering that makes the gemstones appear to be mossy, banded, or contain tiny branching trees. Some geodes, thundereggs, and limb casts are filled with varying types of agate.

JASPER

A variety of chalcedony that is opaque (light does not pass through it) and, like agate, is quite variable. Red and yellow jasper are most common, but some areas have blue, green, brown, and even purple jaspers. Jasper thundereggs are also locally common in parts of central Oregon. Central Oregon is also home to a unique and abundant variety of blue-and-green stone called vistaite jasper (though it's technically not a jasper).

GEODE

Geodes can form in different ways, but the end result is the same: a geode is a round rock with an often boring-looking exterior, but it has a hollow or semi-hollow interior lined with minerals. The fun of geodes is both finding them and then breaking them open (carefully!), as you never know what you're going to get.

THUNDEREGG

Thundereggs are the state rock of Oregon. Though they can be found throughout the Pacific Northwest, they are most widespread in Oregon. Like geodes, thundereggs are round, usually about the size of a baseball, and have a boring exterior but an extraordinary core. If you find a thunderegg, you'll need to saw it open to see what's inside. Unlike geodes, thundereggs are typically not hollow and are only formed from rhyolitic lava or ash. Their interiors can be filled with agate, jasper, or opal. Sometimes crystals will form in the gaps between layers.

OPAL

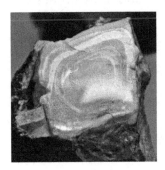

Opal is technically not a mineral because it doesn't have a crystalline structure like true minerals, even though it is made mostly of silica (which is also the primary component of quartz). In the Pacific Northwest, opal occurs in many different varieties. Opal-filled thundereggs and opalized wood are also fairly common in some areas. Opal in our area can be opaque, translucent, and transparent, and the most sought-after varieties are those with iridescent spots of color such as the fire opals at Spencer Opal Mine in Clark County, Idaho. This region of Idaho is often referred to as the Opal Capital of America.

PETRIFIED WOOD

Petrified wood is a form of fossil. Wood is especially good at fossilizing because it is relatively tough, and even after much of it decomposes, the hard internal structure usually remains. This makes an excellent template for mineralization. Petrified wood is prized because it retains the fine details of the plant in life, such as tree rings, knots, bark, and even individual cells. Petrified wood can be found throughout the Pacific Northwest and appears in white, black, brown, and even green varieties. Sometimes the wood is replaced with agate (agatized) or opal (opalized). These are most common in small limb casts (see next page).

ASSEMBLING A COLLECTION OF MINERALS & GEMS

LIMB CASTS

When layers and layers of hot ash encase a piece of wood, they create a detailed impression of the surface of the wood, but burn out the interior. These casts act like a mold and are later filled with agate or opal. Unlike petrified wood, the internal structure of limb casts is not usually present. Some of the most prized limb casts are found in central Oregon at Hampton Butte, where they are filled by a unique green agate.

OBSIDIAN

Obsidian is a volcanic glass and technically not a mineral because, like opal, it does not have a crystalline structure. Like glass, it is brittle and it chips and shatters easily and should be handled like you would handle broken glass. **Handle with care!** Typically obsidian is black and shiny, but some samples contain iridescent bubbles and layers giving them gold, rainbow, or fire sheens. There are few sites to reliably collect obsidian in Washington and Idaho, but the Newberry Volcano region of Oregon is world-famous for its obsidian. **Note:** Collecting is not allowed in the Newberry National Volcanic Monument, but Glass Butte is only a few miles away and collecting is encouraged!

INVERTEBRATE FOSSILS

Hard-shelled invertebrates are some of the most commonly fossilized animals. Here in the Pacific Northwest, we can find just about any small animal with a shell or exoskeleton in our fossil record. Things like mollusks (snails, nautiluses, clams) and arthropods (crabs, trilobites, insects) are most common. Our region also has many famous fossil sites for vertebrate animals, such as the John Day Fossil Beds in Oregon and the Hagerman Horse Quarry in Idaho, but vertebrate fossil specimens are protected. If you find something that you think might be a vertebrate fossil, leave it be and report it to a ranger or paleontologist.

PLANT FOSSILS

Plant fossils are common throughout the Pacific Northwest and have been used to tell us a lot about the ancient climate of our region. *Metasequoia* fossils (Dawn redwood), found at the John Day Fossil Beds, are the state fossil of Oregon. Surprisingly, these fossils were discovered in Japan before scientists stumbled upon a small grove of living *Metase-quoia* trees in China. The Chinese botanists who made the discovery were amazed to see a "**living fossil**" that should have gone **extinct** 65 million years ago alive and well in 1945. In our area, the most abundant plant fossils are between 70 and 30 million years old and indicate that the Pacific Northwest used to be a much warmer place during that time.

QUICK QUIZ

Aside from fossils and limb casts, which two rocks on this list are technically not minerals?

_____

_____

Answer on page 140!

Rock and mineral collection

TESTING THE HARDNESS OF MINERALS

Hardness is a useful way to help identify your mineral finds. The **Mohs Hardness Scale**, on the right, ranks some common minerals in terms of hardness, or how easily they can be scratched. Talc, the lowest mineral on the scale, is so soft you can scratch it with your fingers. Diamond is famous for being one of the hardest minerals, and for good reason: almost no natural substances can scratch it.

Making your own hardness test kit is a good way to start learning hands-on with rocks and minerals. Determining a mineral's hardness is a good first step in trying to identify it.

The way the scale works is simple: any material lower on the scale can be scratched by materials above it. So gypsum can scratch talc, but talc can't scratch gypsum. Similarly, calcite, which is a 3, can scratch gypsum *and* talc.

WHAT YOU'LL NEED

Using the scale to test your finds usually goes like this: You find a mineral (not a rock!) and you're not sure what it is. You start out by trying to scratch it with your fingernail. If it leaves a scratch, then it's softer than 2.5 on the scale. Chances are, however, it won't leave a scratch. So you need to move up to a different piece of equipment with a known hardness.

Here are some common, easy-to-find examples:

• Fingernail: 2.5

• A real piece of copper (not a penny, as these coins aren't made of much copper anymore): 3

• Steel nail or a knife: 5.5–6 (for safety reasons, you should have an adult help you with these tests)

• A piece of quartz: 7

Talc
$Mg_3Si_4O_{10}(OH)_2$

Gypsum
$CaSO_4 \cdot 2H_2O$

Calcite
$CaCO_3$

Fluorite
CaF_2

Apatite
$Ca_5(PO_4)_3(F,Cl,OH)$

WHAT TO DO

To scratch it, you need to hold the to-be-scratched mineral firmly in one hand, and use a pointed area of the "scratching" mineral and press firmly, away from your body or fingers. If it leaves a scratch mark, it's softer than the "scratching" mineral. Obviously, for safety reasons you should make sure you have an adult conduct the actual scratch tests—don't handle a knife or a nail yourself.

Once you've found something that scratches it, you're pretty close to figuring out its hardness. Then it's just a matter of scratching it with other minerals from the chart or your scratching tools then seeing if you can figure out an even more specific range. Once you've narrowed down the hardness some more, looking up mineral hardness is easy online.

Note: You can also buy lab-calibrated "hardness pick" kits; these are much more accurate, but they can be expensive.

Keep track of your hardness tests here. Doing so can help you learn to identify your finds!

_____

_____

_____

_____

_____

_____

_____

Orthoclase
$KAlSi_3O_8$

Quartz
SiO_2

Topaz
$Al_2SiO_4(F,OH)_2$

Corundum
Al_2O_3

Diamond
C

LOOKING AT SOIL, DIRT, OR A DEAD LOG

WHY DOES DIRT MATTER?

When was the last time you took a good long look at dirt? You might think that it's not all that interesting to look at, but dirt is the lifeblood of a forest. It's full of fungi, small insects and invertebrates, **dormant** seeds, incubating eggs of all kinds (from slugs to bugs to lizards!), and it provides the nutrients for every living thing in the forest. Nearly all plants, with the help of tiny fungi in their roots, absorb nutrients and water from the soil and make sugars from sunlight. All those sugars and nutrients get consumed by herbivores, like caterpillars, deer, and grasshoppers. Then those herbivores get consumed by other animals, like raccoons, birds, and us! Then, when those animals die, their bodies decompose and their nutrients return to the soil. It's the circle of life, and dirt plays a very important role.

Take a look at the dirt in a forest near you, and you might be surprised by what you find. Try using a magnifying lens, a macro mode on a camera, or a microscope to get a closer look at the organisms living in soil!

WHAT TO DO

A dead log might look, well, dead, but it's actually its own little world. Insects, such as wasps, burrow into the wood to lay their eggs. Under the

Millipede

bark, ants and beetles are busy tunneling or making a home (they often leave behind intricate patterns on the wood), and it's easy to spot tiny mushrooms and sometimes very colorful slime molds, which are often food sources for other animals, such as slugs, snails, and insects. Once you start looking closely, it's easy to find a lot more to like than you might expect.

Safety Note: If you have venomous spiders or snakes in your area, make sure you go out with an adult and take proper precautions (wear gloves, long pants, etc.) when digging in dirt or turning over logs.

Tiny mushroom

WHAT YOU MIGHT SEE

- Slugs or tiny land snails

- Isopods (also called rolly-pollies or pillbugs)

- Lichen (an organism that consists of algae and/or bacteria and fungi, all living together)

- Slime molds

- Spiders

- Ants

- Springtails (tiny insect-like animals that can spring away from danger)

Springtail

QUICK QUESTIONS

1. How many types of life did you find?

_____

_____

2. Were you able to identify them all?

_____

MAKE A SELF-PORTRAIT USING NATURE

WHAT YOU WILL NEED

• Several blank pieces of paper

• A glue stick, if you want to create a permanent piece of art

WHAT TO DO

With an adult, start out by gathering some materials from nature with interesting shapes, colors, and sizes. Look for twigs, fallen leaves or pine needles, cones, seeds, flowers or petals, flakes of bark, feathers, or blades of grass. Anything that is relatively flat, light, and dry makes great material for your nature "painting."

Next, it's time to get creative! Do you want to paint a landscape, or your favorite animal, or perhaps a self-portrait? Start with a large piece of material first. Maybe it can be the body of an Orca whale, or the start of a hill or mountain range. Arrange the materials on your paper until you're satisfied with their shape and design.

You can glue pieces down as you go, or, once you're done, you can return the materials back to where you found them. The wildlife in your backyard will thank you.

GEOLOGY & GEMSTONES CROSSWORD

ACROSS

4. A fossil species of tree that was once thought extinct; later, living trees of this genus were discovered in China.

5. Technically not a mineral (usually black)

8. The state rock of Oregon

9. Usually hollow inside and lined with crystals

DOWN

1. A variety of chalcedony that is opaque

2. Technically not a mineral (usually white)

3. Often preserves the grain and growth rings

6. The state gemstone of Oregon

7. A variety of chalcedony that is translucent

Answers on page 141!

SPOTTING THE MOON, THE PLANETS & ORION

In winter, it can be hard to stay active outside. After all, it's cold and it gets dark early, but for stargazers, winter is one of the best seasons around. There aren't any bugs, you don't have to stay up late for it to get really dark, and some of the best constellations are visible during the winter. So if you dress up warmly, grab a lawn chair, and bust out a small telescope or binoculars, you can see the planets, the moon, and even the Orion Nebula and the Pleiades star cluster.

WHAT YOU WILL NEED

- Warm clothes

- A lawn chair

- A small telescope or, if you don't have one, binoculars

- A field guide and/or virtual planetarium software like Stellarium (which is free for Windows computers and Macs)

WHAT TO DO

First, figure out what you want to see before you head out. That's where a good field guide comes in. Virtual planetarium software is great too, because it can show you exactly what the sky will look like wherever you are (and whenever you want).

Starting with the moon is always a good idea, as it's bright and impossible to miss when it's up. The best time to observe the moon is in the "first quarter" when only one-half of the moon is lit up, as it reveals a lot more detail than a full moon, when all that reflected sunlight washes out the view. If you have a small telescope, try holding a smartphone over the eyepiece, and see if you can snap some pictures. This can be tricky, but if you take a bunch of pictures and fiddle with the settings, you can get some wonderful shots (there are also phone mounts you can buy fairly inexpensively online, though you have to get the right model for your phone).

After you take a look at the moon, make sure you get a chance to see Jupiter, Saturn, Mars, and Venus. You'll need to refer to your field guide

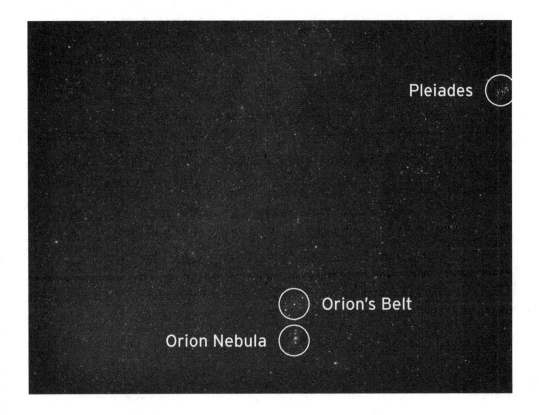

Pleiades

Orion's Belt

Orion Nebula

or planetarium software for when and where to look for each, because they appear to move through the sky over time. Still, it's worth the effort: seeing Saturn's rings for the first time will make you gasp.

Note: Don't expect to see the rings like you would in a picture from NASA—the planets will look pretty darn small. But if you're patient and you focus just right, you'll see the planets *for real*. It's an amazing experience. Even if you just have binoculars, you can often spot Jupiter's largest moons: Io, Europa, Ganymede, and Callisto.

Finally, even if you only have a small telescope or binoculars, make sure to take a look at the constellation Orion. Easy to spot throughout much of the late fall and winter, it's famous for Orion's Belt, a line of three evenly spaced stars at the center of the constellation. If you look just below the belt, you'll see a star that looks a bit smudged; it's actually not a star at all. It's a nebula, an area where stars are forming. Viewed through binoculars or a small telescope, it's a wonderful sight. The same is true for the Pleiades, a bright star cluster. To find it, simply follow from Orion's Belt up and to the right. If you're just looking with your eyes, it looks like a little smudge, but through binoculars or a telescope, it looks kind of like a miniature version of the Big Dipper.

View through binoculars

BIRDS IN YOUR BIOME

Birds can be found in every habitat on Earth—from the mountains to the coasts; in the most remote wilderness; and in the middle of the city. And every habitat has its own unique types of birds! Learning to recognize these animals is a challenging scientific task. But that makes it all the more rewarding when you succeed. Below, we've provided a brief guide to some of the Pacific Northwest's most common and most famous bird inhabitants. Learn more about your biome on page 6. What birds are you most likely to see in your area?

COMMON CITY BIRDS

Mallard

Red-tailed Hawk

Northern Flicker

Mourning Dove

American Crow

American Robin

Black-capped Chickadee

European Starling

TEMPERATE RAINFOREST, COASTLINES, AND WET WESTERN VALLEYS

Rhinoceros Auklet

Marbled Murrelet

Black
Oystercatcher

Marbled Godwit

Sooty Grouse

Bald Eagle

Rufous
Hummingbird

Red-breasted
Sapsucker

Steller's Jay

Varied Thrush

Chestnut-backed
Chickadee

Hermit Warbler

BIRDS IN YOUR BIOME

CONIFEROUS FORESTS AND EASTERN MOUNTAINS

Great Gray Owl

Dusky Grouse

Harlequin Duck

Calliope Hummingbird

Lewis's Woodpecker

Red-naped Sapsucker

Canada Jay

Clark's Nutcracker

Pygmy Nuthatch

Mountain Bluebird

Mountain Chickadee

Pine Grosbeak

DRY SHRUBLANDS, DESERTS, AND EASTERN LOWLANDS

Rough-legged Hawk

Prairie Falcon

Greater Sage Grouse

California Quail

Black-chinned Hummingbird

Say's Phoebe

Sage Thrasher

Sagebrush Sparrow

Vesper Sparrow

Lazuli Bunting

Bullock's Oriole

Yellow-headed Blackbird

MAKE YOUR YARD BIRD-FRIENDLY

Lawns are pretty, but they don't do a lot to help birds, bugs, and most other kinds of wildlife. To really draw birds (and the insects they often eat!) to your yard, you need to make your yard a bit wilder. It's pretty easy to start doing this. Here are a few tips to get going:

PLANT NATIVE PLANTS

Whether you're planting native trees that provide cover, nesting sites, or fruit, or flowers that attract hummingbirds and grow seeds, native plants are beacons to birds. For a list of what to plant, visit: www.audubon.org/native-plants. To make sure you're finding the best native plants, look for a native plant nursery near you.

PUT OUT A WATER SOURCE

If you live in drier habitats east of the Cascades, birds (and other wildlife!) are often more attracted to water than they are to food and native plants. A bird bath, especially one with a "water wiggler" (available at many birding or home improvement stores) is a great option! The movement of the water helps to prevent mosquitoes from laying eggs in the water. If you place your water source on the ground, you'll attract other thirsty animals too, like rabbits, chipmunks, and lizards. Don't forget to put a rock or ramp in the water to help prevent small animals and baby birds from drowning!

DON'T SPRAY YOUR YARD WITH BUG OR WEED KILLERS

Mosquitoes are sure annoying, but the popular "foggers" or sprays that many people apply to their yards don't just kill mosquitoes. These broad-spectrum insecticides often kill any bugs they touch, including bees, butterflies, and the many beetles or other creepy-crawlies that birds depend on for food. Pesticides can also directly harm birds, too.

Baldhip Rose

Salmonberry

Evening Grosbeak

Common Willow Calligrapher Beetle

LEAVE OUT NEST-MAKING MATERIALS IN SPRING

Bird nests are pretty incredible, and it's even more impressive that birds make them using only their feet and their beaks!

WHAT TO DO

You can help them out by leaving natural, pesticide-free nesting materials in handy locations around your yard. Examples include soft, fluffy plant parts, such as the down from cattails or cottonwoods, moss, or feathers you find on the ground (but make sure to wear gloves when picking those up). You can situate those in easy-to-access places around your yard: on the ground, wedged into tree bark, or even hanging in an empty suet feeder.

Important Note: There are some things you don't want to give to birds, especially manmade or synthetic products such as plastic, metal, or lint. These can be **toxic** to birds, either if they eat some of them, or if they absorb some of the chemicals in them.

Cattail down is often used in bird nests.

MAKE A RECIPE TO FEED TO BIRDS

If you get creative, you can feed birds a lot more than birdseed! Making your own bird food is a fun way to attract the birds you want to see.

Here are two options, although there are lots of others.

DO-IT-YOURSELF BIRDSEED MIX

A lot of the birdseed mixes sold in stores just aren't very good. Often, they contain lots of filler seeds (such as milo, a small, brown, round seed). Filler seeds don't have a lot of the nutrients that birds need, unlike seeds such as black oil sunflower seeds, which are full of good stuff like protein, vitamins, and fats.

So what do you do? Make your own birdseed mix! Buy some black oil sunflower seeds to use as your base, then add other seeds to those.

Here's a mix that works great for platform feeders. All of the ingredients are usually available at garden centers or home improvement stores.

WHAT YOU'LL NEED

• 4 cups black oil sunflower seeds

• 1 cup peanut chips

• 1 cup cracked corn

WHAT TO DO

Mix it all together and place it on a hanging bird feeder. For an extra-tasty treat, you can also add in some sliced apples or plums.

A SIMPLE PEANUT BUTTER BIRDSEED FEEDER

WHAT YOU'LL NEED

- Pine cones

- Peanut butter

- Black oil sunflower seeds or a birdseed mix

- Some string

WHAT TO DO

This tried-and-true recipe really works. First, you'll need to collect some pine cones. Then mix some peanut butter and sunflower seeds in a bowl. Next, take the pine cones and push them into the peanut butter and seeds, making sure everything is mixed together well like in the picture. Now tie some string to the top of each pine cone, and hang it from a tree. You can do this as many times as you'd like.

If you can't find any pine cones, just mix the ingredients together, and then "paint" or smear the mixture onto a tree's bark.

Make both kinds of feeders, then keep track of the birds that come to each one! Did different birds come to the different feeders?

_____

_____

_____

_____

DO A BACKYARD BIRD COUNT

If you're new to birding, chances are you probably haven't conducted a backyard bird count before. It's a simple activity, but it can teach you and your friends quite a bit about birds, including how to recognize their calls and when and where to look. It's also a lot of fun, and you might be surprised at what you find. Best of all, you don't need any gear at all, though a field guide to birds, binoculars, and a smartphone camera are handy.

WHAT YOU'LL NEED

• A notepad and a pen or pencil, to record your finds

• A field guide, binoculars, and a smartphone camera (optional)

WHAT TO DO

To conduct your count, give each participant a notebook, and pick a 15-minute time slot to look for birds. Go to your backyard, or even a balcony, and quietly look, and listen, for birds. Look near feeders, if you have them; see if you can spy birds flitting about in cover or perched in trees, and especially near garden areas (even potted plants or container gardens sometimes have house finches and the like in them). Wherever you are, but especially in the city or the suburbs, look for birds soaring overhead. (The cities might not seem like birding hot spots, but because major cities are often by rivers and usually have plenty of pigeons and other prey, they are often home to nesting populations of peregrine falcons and the like.)

When someone spots a bird, point it out—again, quietly—and try to snag a zoomed-in shot. (It doesn't have to be perfect, just enough to help with identification.) Then record what kind of birds they are, if you recognize them, how many birds you spotted, and what they were doing. If you don't recognize a bird and didn't get a picture of it, sketch out a quick drawing or make notes about its appearance, color, and size. You can then consult a field guide or photos online to try to identify it.

BIRD CALLS

You may hear a bird without seeing it—and this will happen more than you'd think. If you recognize the call, mark it down and add it to your count. If you don't know the call (again, this will happen pretty often), head online after your count to a website like All About Birds (www.allaboutbirds.org), and listen to recordings of birds that could help you figure it out.

RECORD YOUR FINDS

After you're done counting birds for 15 minutes, combine all of your finds into a list, and then consider setting up an account on a community science site such as eBird. There, you can create a "life list" of species spotted over time, and you'll also contribute to science—the resulting maps help create a snapshot of bird life over time.

DO A BACKYARD BIRD COUNT

THE CHRISTMAS BIRD COUNT

Once you get the hang of doing a bird count, consider participating in a national one. There are two long-running bird counts. One is the Christmas Bird Count, which has been around for 120 years. It takes place from mid-December to early January, and volunteers spread out to count birds in specific areas around each state and the country, with counts occurring in each local area for only one day. (So if you want to join in on the fun, tell your parents and prepare ahead of time!) To find out more, visit www.audubon.org /conservation/science/christmas-bird-count.

THE GREAT BACKYARD BIRD COUNT

This bird count is similar to the Christmas Bird Count, but it takes place everywhere, and you can participate if you spot birds for as little as 15 minutes, making it easy to join. It takes place in February. For more information and to sign up, visit www.birdcount.org.

Keep track of the birds you see or spot here!

_____

_____

_____

_____

_____

_____

DATE: _____
LOCATION: _____

DATE: Feb 2, 2020
LOCATION: Jackson Bottom Wetlands
Washington Co., Hillsboro, OR

Christmas Bird Count:

Canada Goose   5
Tundra Swan   2
Northern Shoveler   12
Mallard   8
Northern Pintail   6
Green-winged Teal   3
Anna's Hummingbird   1
___ Blue Heron   2
___ Robin   7

PLANT A HUMMINGBIRD, BEE & BUTTERFLY GARDEN

One way you can help wildlife wherever you live is by making your area a bit wilder. The easiest way to do that is to plant native plants. You don't need a huge amount of space to do this; even a small container garden with native plants can help attract—and feed—pollinators.

WHAT TO DO

Here are a few examples of how to attract some of the more sought-after pollinators:

- Flowering shrubs are some of the best plants to include in your yard or garden because they not only provide flowers, but they also provide hiding places for birds and insects. Depending on your area, consider planting rhododendrons, Syringa (Mock Orange), Red-osier Dogwood, *Arctostaphylos* (madrone or manzanita), *Spiraea*, or Chokecherry.

- For smaller gardens, wildflowers might be a better option. To attract hummingbirds, try planting Wild Bergamot, columbine, Pacific Bleeding Heart, penstemon, or Scarlet Gilia. If you have space for a vine, Orange Honeysuckle is a favorite of all hummingbirds.

- Other pollinators are usually less picky than hummingbirds and will be attracted to any part of your garden or yard that produces a lot of flowers all season long. Try to plant a variety of flower shapes and colors and find plants that produce many small flowers. Consider planting native Purple Sage, Giant Hyssop, native coneflowers, Yarrow, lupine, American Vetch, native onion, American Cow Parsnip, or biscuitroot. Any kind of native daisy, aster, or blanket flower is also ideal.

- Let the "weeds" be: Dandelions, Common Blue Violets, and plants like White Clover provide bees, butterflies, and other beneficial insects with needed resources. Not only are

Clockwise from top: Hydaspe Fritillary on Giant Hyssop, sweat bee on Yarrow, Rufous Hummingbird

these plants pretty and great to walk on (clover doesn't get crunchy like turfgrass does), they're tough and they don't need much care at all.

Try a hummingbird feeder: Hummingbirds, even in the middle of the city, will seek out hummingbird feeders and visit them regularly. Mix a sugar-water combination with 1 cup of sugar for every 4 cups of water. No need to add any food coloring to the water—the hummingbirds will be attracted to the red or yellow perches or fake flowers at the base of the feeder. Be sure to refill the container regularly, but consider taking down the feeder in the fall to encourage stubborn birds to migrate.

For an excellent list of native flowers that are ideal for attracting native pollinators, check out these region-specific recommendations from the Xerces Society: https://xerces.org /pollinator-conservation/pollinator-friendly-plant-lists.

SET UP A
WINDOW FEEDER

If you want to get an up-close look at birds, put up a window feeder. These transparent ledge-style feeders attach to the window via suction cups, and once the birds get used to the feeder and your presence on the other side of the glass, birds will chow down, enabling you to watch them from almost no distance at all.

BIRD NEST-CAMS

For a different kind of up-close look at birds, head online and look at the many different nest-cams offered on various bird sites. There are online nest-cams for eagles hawks, ospreys, even hummingbirds.

For a list, visit www.allaboutbirds.org/cams.

MAKE YOUR WINDOWS SAFER FOR BIRDS

Hundreds of millions of birds are killed or injured each year when they accidentally fly into windows, often because they saw a reflection of nearby plants or the sky and thought it was a safe place to fly.

WHAT TO DO

There are a few simple safety steps you can take to help:

1. Close your blinds or curtains—this will make the window look more like a barrier. This is very important at night.

2. Put anti-collision window decals on your windows. These help reduce the reflective surfaces that can confuse birds. They're not 100% effective, but making your own can be a fun craft activity! You can even make different decals for your favorite holidays (bats for Halloween!) or for the changing seasons (snowflakes for winter!).

3. When placing bird feeders, either keep them well away from a window (more than 20 feet) or keep them very close to a window (on the window, via suction cups, or just few feet away). Even if a bird flies into a window from a close-by feeder, it won't be moving fast enough to hurt itself.

4. Place ribbons, pinwheels, and other moving accessories in front of windows to scare birds away.

5. Consider purchasing the many other products specifically designed to prevent window collisions.

WILDLIFE REHABILITATION
NEAR YOU

If you see an animal get hurt or find one that you know is injured, keep your pets indoors and then contact your local wildlife rehabilitation center or a permit-carrying wildlife rehabilitation expert. To find one, visit the website of your state's natural resources department.

WHAT TO DO

If you find what you think is an orphaned baby animal and it's in a safe spot, don't pick it up. Instead, call your local wildlife rehabilitation center first—the animal might not actually be orphaned at all (its parents may be nearby or gathering food), and handling or disturbing the animal might actually harm it. When in doubt, just leave the animal alone and call an expert.

This Dark-eyed Junco was trapped in a garage and released unharmed.

Have you ever encountered an injured animal? What happened to it? Were you able to help it? Write your story here.

_____

_____

_____

_____

_____

_____

_____

_____

_____

_____

_____

_____

_____

_____

_____

MAMMALS

Mammals, like us, are any animal that has hair, gives birth to live young instead of laying eggs, and nurses their babies with milk. The Pacific Northwest is home to more species of mammals than any other region in the United States! We have more than 100 species of land mammals, like the Pronghorn, Cascade Golden-mantled Ground Squirrel, and the Spotted Bat, and over 30 species of marine mammals including Orcas, Harbor Seals, and Gray Whales.

Cascade Golden-mantled Ground Squirrel

Elk (Wapiti)

Gray Whale

Pronghorn

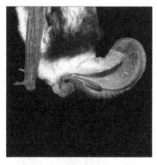
Spotted Bat

Red Squirrel

Sagebrush Vole

River Otter

The Pacific Northwest is home to several species of unique mammals that can be found nowhere else in the world. The Olympic Marmot, for example, is only found in montane (mountain) meadows in the Olympic Peninsula above 4000 feet. When an animal is unique to one specific area of the world, we say that it is endemic to that region. There are several other species of mammals that are endemic to the Pacific Northwest including several ground squirrels, voles, moles, and shrews.

Olympic Marmot

Pygmy Rabbit

Northern Idaho Ground Squirrel

QUICK QUIZ

There are six official state symbols of the Pacific Northwest that are mammals. Can you name them all? Hint: Two are extinct!

_____

_____

_____

_____

_____

Answers on page 140!

IDENTIFYING MAMMAL TRACKS

Have you ever been walking near a river, pond, or beach and noticed animal tracks in the sand? Did you know that mammalogists can identify the animal that created those tracks? It's a skill that you can learn too!

WHERE TO FIND MAMMAL TRACKS

The best places to find clear, well-preserved mammal tracks are in slightly muddy soil, wet sand, dusty earth, or just after a light dusting of snow. Think about what areas of your backyard or neighborhood might have these ideal conditions. Slightly muddy soil is common near bodies of water, but you can also search a baseball field after it rains, or a well-watered garden bed. If you live near a sandy beach, look for tracks in the area between the surf and the dry sand. In the Pacific Northwest east of the Cascades, most sunny trails are coated in a fine layer of dust, which preserves even the smallest mammal tracks.

HOW TO IDENTIFY MAMMAL TRACKS

Start by thinking about how big the tracks are. Do they look more like the size of squirrel feet or the feet of a big dog? Next, count the number of toes. Dogs (including coyotes, wolves, and foxes) and cats (including bobcats, lynx, and mountain lions) only have four toes that touch the ground when they walk, while skunks, opossums, weasels, raccoons, and bears all have five. Rodents like mice, rats, squirrels, and marmots show a variety of 4-toed and 5-toed prints.

Next, look at the space in between the toes. Can you see any signs of fur or webbing between the toes? What about at the tip of the toes? Can you see any indentations from claws? Most mammals, including dogs, rodents, weasels, bears, and raccoons, will make claw marks on the ground when they walk in mud, sand, or snow that is at least a half an inch deep. Cats (including bobcats, mountain lions, etc.) have retractable claws and rarely leave claw indentations when they walk.

Finally, compare the tracks you're investigating to images of tracks in the guide on the following pages. Remember to keep in mind the size, number of toes, and whether or not you see webbing, claws, or fur. The most common tracks you'll find in areas near large populations of humans are domestic dogs and cats as well as raccoons, skunks, squirrels, and mice.

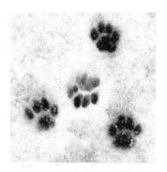

Cats don't leave claw marks when they walk.

Deer prints alongside a boot print makes a good size comparison.

QUICK QUESTIONS

1. How many toe prints should you look for on a deer track?

_____

2. Where do animals with webbed toes tend to live? Do you know of any mammals that live in those habitats that might have big webbed feet? Hint: It's a state symbol of Oregon!

_____

DOGS & CATS

DOMESTIC DOG
Canis familiaris

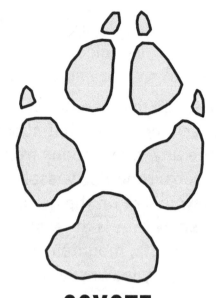

COYOTE
Canis latrans

RED FOX
Vulpes vulpes

DOMESTIC CAT
Felis catus

BOBCAT
Lynx rufus

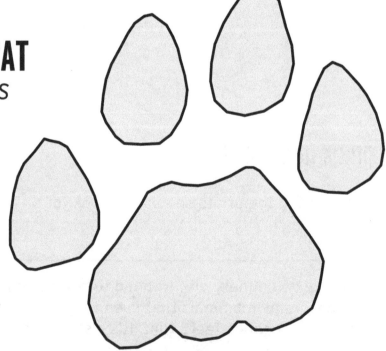

MOUNTAIN LION
Puma concolor

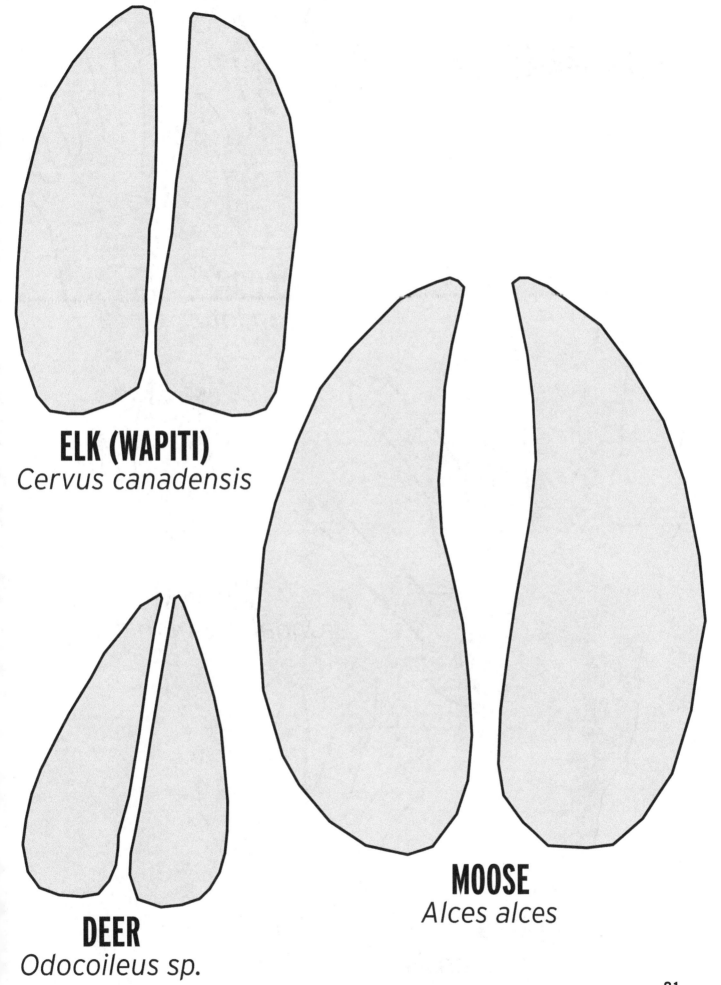

ELK (WAPITI)
Cervus canadensis

DEER
Odocoileus sp.

MOOSE
Alces alces

RIVER MAMMALS

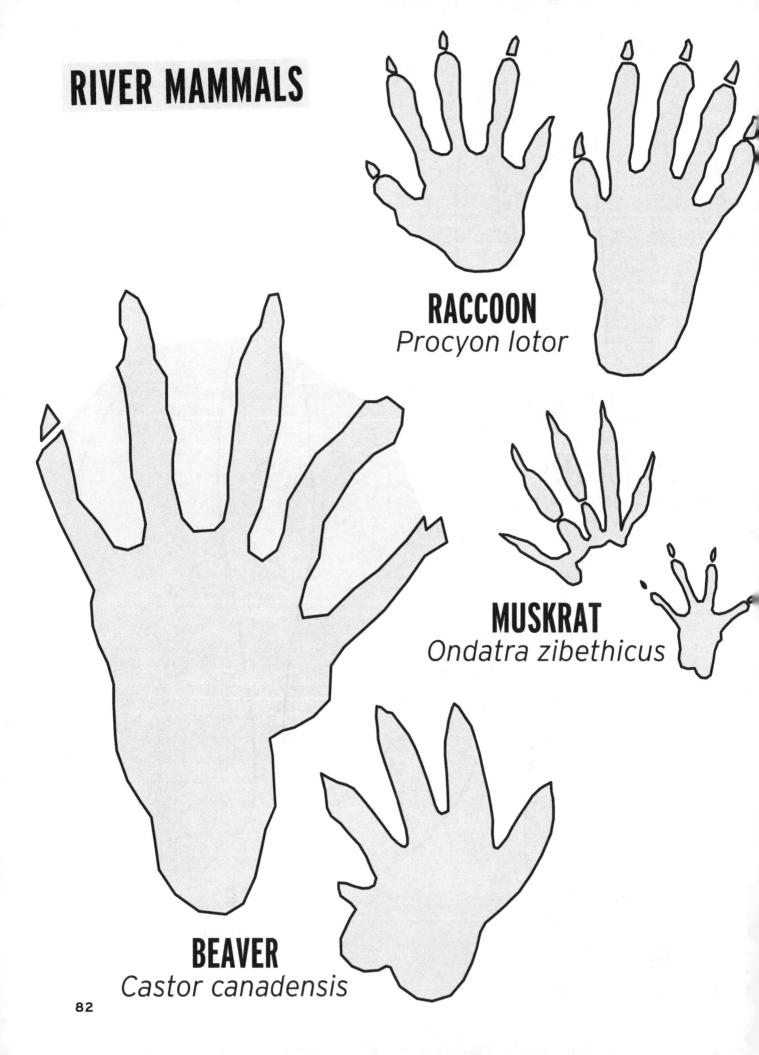

RACCOON
Procyon lotor

MUSKRAT
Ondatra zibethicus

BEAVER
Castor canadensis

STRIPED SKUNK
Mephitis mephitis

RIVER OTTER
Lontra canadensis

AMERICAN MINK
Neovison vison

LONG-TAILED WEASEL
Mustela frenata

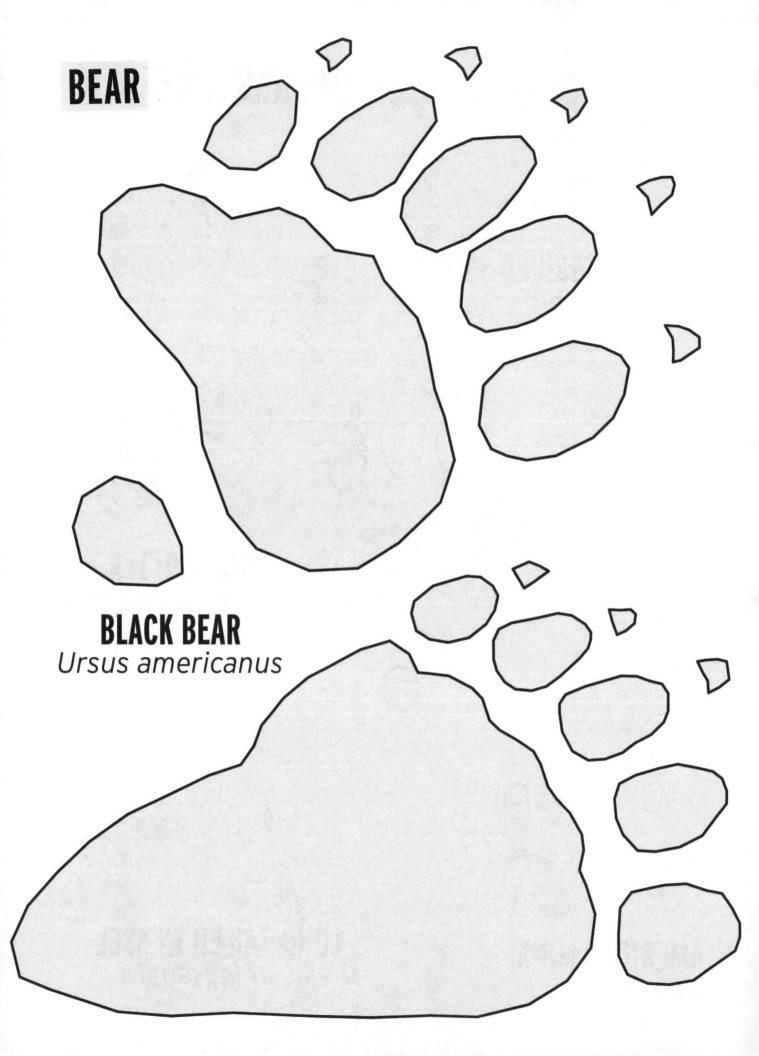

BEAR

BLACK BEAR
Ursus americanus

MAKE YOUR OWN TRACKS

Humans are mammals too! So you should put your own tracks into this guide! Trace the outline of your hand or foot (or both!) in the space provided. How do your tracks compare to the American Black Bear? What tracks look most like yours?

LEARNING TO IDENTIFY BASIC GROUPS OF BUGS

If you want to learn about insects, start by learning to identify the basic groups (or orders) of insects. All insects have 6 legs, 3 body segments, and usually 1 or 2 sets of wings. Some, such as butterflies and moths, you might already know, but there are quite a few more to discover. This list isn't all-inclusive, but it gives you a fun idea of some of the insects you can find!

ANTS, BEES & WASPS (HYMENOPTERA)

Ichneumon Wasps

Gall Wasps

Yellowjackets and Paper Wasps

Spider Wasps

Ants

Mining Bees

Sweat Bees

Bumblebees and Honeybees

BUTTERFLIES & MOTHS (LEPIDOPTERA)

Leafroller Moths

Grass Moths

Plume Moths

Hooktip Moths

Geometer
(Inchworm) Moths

Giant Silkworm
Moths

Sphinx Moths

Tiger and Tussock
Moths

Skippers

Swallowtails

Gossamer-winged
Butterflies

Brushfooted
Butterflies

LEARNING TO IDENTIFY
BASIC GROUPS OF BUGS

BEETLES (COLEOPTERA)

Predatory Ground Beetles

Darkling Beetles

Carrion Beetles

Stag Beetles

Scarabs

Metallic Wood-boring Beetles

Click Beetles

Blister Beetles

Lady Beetles

Longhorn Beetles

Leaf Beetles

Weevils and Bark Beetles

TRUE BUGS (HEMIPTERA)

Stinkbugs

Leafhoppers

Spittlebugs

Box Elder Bugs

Cicadas

Aphids

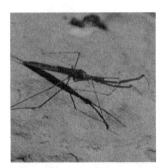
Brown
Waterscorpions

Derbid
Planthoppers

DAMSELFLIES & DRAGONFLIES (ODONATA)

Spreadwing
Damselflies

Pond Damselflies

Darners

Skimmers

LEARNING TO IDENTIFY BASIC GROUPS OF BUGS

FLIES (DIPTERA)

Tachinid Flies

Gnats, Mosquitoes, Midges

Robber Flies

Flower Flies

House Flies, Blow Flies, Dung Flies

Crane Flies

GRASSHOPPERS, CRICKETS, AND KATYDIDS (ORTHOPTERA)

Grasshoppers

Katydids

Crickets

MANTISES (MANTOIDEA)

WALKING STICKS (PHASMIDA)

SNAKEFLIES (RAPHIDIOPTERA)

STONEFLIES (PLECOPTERA)

CADDISFLIES (TRICHOPTERA)

MAYFLIES (EPHEMEROPTERA)

LEARNING TO IDENTIFY
BASIC GROUPS OF BUGS

NON-INSECT LAND ARTHROPODS

Animals with exoskeletons that have more than six legs, more or fewer than three body segments, and no wings.

Orb Weavers

Ground Spiders

Crab Spiders

Jumping Spiders

Harvestmen

Mites and Ticks

Scorpions

Centipedes

Yellow-spotted
Millipedes

Eurasian
Millipedes

Pill Bugs, Rolly-
pollies, Wood Lice

OTHER LAND INVERTEBRATES

Animals with no internal skeleton or external skeleton (exoskeleton).

Roundback Slugs

Banana Slug

Sideband Snail

Banded Wood Snail

Earthworms

QUICK QUIZ

Idaho, Oregon, and Washington each have an official state insect! What group do each of the state insects belong in?

_____

_____

_____

Answers on page 140!

MAKE YOUR YARD A LITTLE WILDER

Many insect populations are at risk. Habitat destruction, insecticide spraying (which kills a lot more than just mosquitoes), and water pollution can all play a role. Lawns, in particular, are part of the problem, as they are incredibly widespread and not all that useful for many plants and animals. That's why it's helpful to make your yard a bit wilder.

WHAT TO DO

Here's a checklist of things you and your family can do to make a corner of your yard a little wilder and more nature-friendly:

☐ Plant native plants (like those listed for birds on Audubon's website here: www.audubon.org/native-plants)

☐ Don't spray broad-spectrum pesticides or herbicides

☐ Leave a patch of grass unmowed

☐ Don't pull up the dandelions (even though they're **non-native**, they attract a lot of neat bugs)

☐ Don't rake dead leaves

☐ Leave out logs and sticks

☐ Make a bee house (more information below)

Over time, keep track of the critters you find in this wild corner, and compare it to the rest of your yard. You'll find that even a small patch of plants can attract critters you may have never seen before.

Most native bees do not make big hives like honeybees. Instead, they make their home for one or a few baby bees in a small hole in the ground, on a tree, or on a log. Most bees can't make these small holes on their own and need to find ones that were already made by other animals. We can help by constructing a bee house with plenty of holes of different sizes for many different kinds of native bees.

A simple bee house

The simplest bee houses are just logs with holes drilled at various sizes and depths. Smaller logs with only four or five holes are excellent because they are less work to clean and replace each year (see below). More complex bee "hotels" are made of many smaller logs or wood blocks with additional hollow reeds or paper straws in between. We recommend avoiding these larger structures because they are more difficult to maintain and tend to attract more fungi, **parasites**, and **predators**. Individual nest holes should have a diameter between ⅛ and ½" and a depth between 4 and 6" (6" is ideal), and they should not go all the way through the log.

Once you have holes drilled in your log, mount it firmly to a tree, fence post, or the side of your house approximately 3 to 5' above the ground in a location where it will stay dry and receive morning sun. In the winter, if you get snow in your area, bring the bee house into an unheated garage until March, when the babies will want to leave their nests. Then, towards the end of summer, clean out each of the holes (re-drill any, if necessary) and remount the bee house so that it is ready for new occupants. If you'd like to make your drill holes easier to clean out each year, try lining them with parchment paper and simply replacing the linings each year.

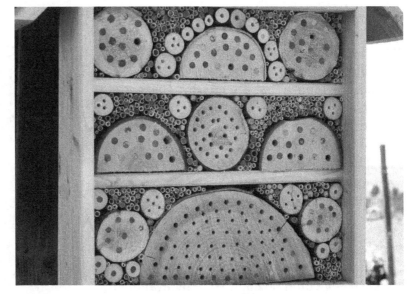

An elaborate bee hotel

RAISE NATIVE CATERPILLARS & RELEASE THEM

Finding a caterpillar is one of the highlights of spring and summer. But unless it's a really well-known caterpillar, like a Monarch, identifying caterpillars can be tricky for beginners. Many caterpillars, including all of the classic inchworms, will actually end up being moths. Even the name scientists use for these moths—Geometridae—is a reference to geometry and how these caterpillars "measure" as they walk.

But you don't need to identify your caterpillar to rear it; after all, one of the most fun ways to identify a moth or a butterfly is after it's turned into an adult!

WHAT YOU'LL NEED

- A butterfly house (it's best to purchase a high-quality one online first)
- An ample supply of fresh leaves
- A water source for the leaves, but one that the caterpillar can't enter (pill bottles work great)

WHAT TO DO

When you find a caterpillar, immediately note what plant you find it on or, if it's on the ground, the plants that are nearby. These are likely the caterpillar's host plants (the ones it needs to eat to become an adult). If you're unsure of which plants to gather, bring in a sampling of several different kinds. If you want an exact answer, post a photo of your caterpillar on a site like BugGuide.net and ask for help on finding out what it eats.

Once you have the caterpillar and the host plants, you'll need to ready your butterfly house. Many common commercially available houses are mesh cylinders.

Western Tent Moth caterpillar

First, you need to prepare your water source for the host plants. Do not provide a water dish or another water source at the bottom of a butterfly house; caterpillars drown easily. Instead, have a parent help you drill or cut a hole in a small container like an old pill bottle, and put the plant stems into the water source (but make sure the caterpillar can't fall into the water and drown).

Over time, you'll need to replace the leaves, and clean up its poop (known as frass). Eventually, the caterpillar will begin to pupate. This is a fascinating process in its own right, but watching one emerge is even better.

Of course, things can go wrong when collecting wild caterpillars: parasitic wasps often attack or infest caterpillars; if your cage is dirty, they can get sick; and if you find a caterpillar in late summer, it might be one that overwinters as a pupa. Still, with practice, there's a good chance that you'll get to watch moths and butterflies all summer long if you work at it hard enough!

Tent moths live in silk tents!

An adult Western Tent Moth

GET TO KNOW THE PACIFIC NORTHWEST'S NATIVE BEES

If you've been following the news, you know that bee populations are in trouble. But you're probably most familiar with honeybees, which are actually an **introduced** species native to Europe, not the US. Think of honeybees as farm animals. The honeybees you see in your yard? In a sense, those are kind of like escaped chickens or cows.

Domesticated honeybee populations have run into trouble over the past few decades due to a combination of factors, including pests (especially the Varroa mite), pesticide use, and habitat loss. These domesticated insects play a critical role in pollinating agricultural crops, especially almonds, blueberries, and cherries.

Honeybees aren't the only bees in the US that are threatened; on the contrary, while honeybees get much of the press, there are thousands of native bee species in the US, and many of them are threatened or endangered due to habitat loss, loss of suitable nesting sites, and the like. They range from the familiar bumblebees that flutter along your flowers to carpenter bees, which bore into wood.

QUICK QUIZ

Which one of these is a bee?

1.
2.
3.

Answer on page 140!

IDENTIFY THE POLLINATORS IN YOUR BACKYARD!

The Oregon Department of Agriculture has an excellent series of photographic guides to backyard bugs at www.odaguides.us/guides

BEES

Honeybees

Bumblebees

Furrow Bees

Metallic Furrow Bees

Sweat Bees

Metallic Sweat Bees

Mining Bees

Metallic Green-Striped Sweat Bees

BEE LOOK-ALIKES

Metallic Cuckoo Wasps

Clearwing Bee Moths

Paper Wasps

Yellowjackets

START AN INSECT COLLECTION

If you love bugs, creating a bug collection can help you observe them up close, but if you're not into killing bugs, there's another option: whenever you're outside observing nature, keep an eye out for insects that are already dead! If a bug is dead, and in reasonably good shape, add it to your collection. You'll be surprised at what you find—butterflies and moths, gorgeous beetles, and so on. (After all, insects don't live all that long.) And if all else fails, a photographic collection works too!

WHAT YOU'LL NEED

- Butterfly net
- Lots of zip-top bags or small vials or jars
- Tweezers
- Pencil
- Small pieces of paper or notecards for labels
- Insect pins

WHAT TO DO

Collect bugs! There are many ways to do this, and you can go about it actively (go out hunting with your net) or passively (pick one up off the windowsill when you notice it). Once you have caught a bug, carefully transfer it to your container (zip-top bag, vial, jar, etc.). Clear containers are best because you can observe your bug before releasing it. If you'd like to keep your bugs permanently, kill them humanely by placing them in the freezer for a few days (some

big moths might need longer). If you plan to collect insects permanently, make sure you make a label for each bug! Write down the date, location, weather information, and information about what kind of plant you found it on, and then place that label inside the container with the bug.

Note: Photographic collections are just as valuable as physical ones! After you've caught a bug, place it in the refrigerator or freezer for a few minutes until it slows down (cold makes insects very sleepy). Then place the insect into a white bowl or onto a plate. Now, take as many pictures as possible before it starts to wake up!

Identify the bugs! Using smartphone apps like iNaturalist or websites like BugGuide, upload a photo of your insect and get a professional's help identifying it. This also turns your bug hobby into a scientific data point! In other words, by identifying an insect in a certain place at a certain time of year, scientists can learn how populations or whole ecosystems are doing. Many of these data points create a scientific snapshot of life in your area!

Learn how to pin an insect! The official methods for pinning insects is different for each type. Look for an online tutorial describing the process! It's usually very simple, but moths and butterflies can be very difficult and may require special tools.

A Western Sculpted Pine Borer waking up in a white cereal bowl

The end result

GO MOTHLIGHTING!

WHAT YOU'LL NEED

- A light, either a normal lantern or a UV lamp (simple blacklights available online work)

- An extension cord

- An old bedsheet or a curtain; light-colored ones are best

- Rope

- Flashlights

- A camera

WHAT TO DO

This activity is best during the summer when it is warm, the air is calm, and the bugs are plentiful. With an adult, find a good spot to find bugs at night; generally, the wilder it is, the better (near woods or streams or lakes), but even the middle of a suburban yard will have all sorts of bugs you've likely never seen.

Tie the rope between two trees or other supports and drape the bedsheet over it like you would if you were drying it. I prefer to have my rope low enough to the ground that I can hold down its edges with big rocks to prevent them from flapping in the breeze (which scares away the bugs!). About an hour before sundown, turn on the light and aim it to shine onto the bedsheet. You should place it close enough to the sheet that bugs will be attracted to it instead of the light itself, but **BEWARE**, some lamps get very hot and could burn your sheet!

Then wait, and make periodic visits to the sheet to see what you find! Heading out with a flashlight in one hand and a

Our setup for National Moth Week

camera in another is an easy way to record your finds (and identify them later).

Once you get a look at the insects you've attracted, wait a while longer and visit again later in the night. (Some of the best bug hunting is late at night.)

Note: When you are observing moths, the light might shine on you and your clothes a bit, so it's possible (though not all that likely) to have moths or other bugs land on you. To avoid this, wear a dark shirt (not one that matches the "moth sheet").

Consider joining National Moth Week! Each year in the last week of July, people from around the country go mothlighting to find and count as many different kinds of moths as possible! Because moths are mostly nocturnal, we don't study them as regularly as butterflies or bees. That is why it's so important to participate in this unique citizen science project. Learn more at nationalmothweek.org

You can use UV lights, but regular ones are just as good.

A couple of bugs from one night of mothlighting: Tortricid Moth (above) and Satin Moth (below)

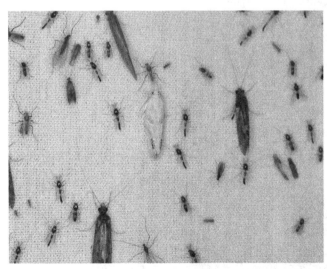

A lot of moths, midges, and caddisflies!

GO TIDE POOLING
OR PIER PEERING!

Ocean life is abundant and diverse. It's always a treat to get the chance to see the ocean's inhabitants up close! If you live near the ocean, a visit to the shore will always introduce you to new, weird, and exciting animals! The best places to see plentiful and interesting ocean life is not the beach, however—it's at the rocky shores, docks, and piers.

WHERE TO GO

Tide pools can be found anywhere near rocky shorelines in the maritime Pacific Northwest. Even on a sandy beach, you can usually spot a nearby rocky area to the north or south. When in doubt, consult the internet for the best places to visit. For Washington's coastline, we'd recommend the Washington State Parks official blog AdventureAwaits.com and for Oregon beaches, we'd recommend Oregon State Parks official guide to tide pools "Tide Pools Are Alive!"

(available at stateparks.oregon.gov) These online resources provide additional information regarding restroom availability, interpretive programming, and parking restrictions. But if you can't make it to the beach, public piers and docks are also great options! (**Note:** Many docks and piers are private property. Observe local signage and do not trespass!)

GET TO KNOW THE TIDES

Tides are the cyclical rise and fall of the oceans caused by the gravity of the moon and sun as the Earth rotates. Most places on the coast see two high tides

and two low tides every day. The exact timing and size of those tides depends on where you are and what day of the year it is. Fortunately, tide tables predicting the exact height and timing of the day's tides can be found online and at most visitor's centers near the ocean. In the Pacific Northwest, the lowest daily low tides occur during the day in the summer and during the night in the winter.

WHEN TO GO

Tide pooling, beachcombing, and pier peering are all best during low-low tides. These happen once per day and last for one or two hours. In the winter, the lowest low-low tides are around midnight, while the lowest low-low tides in the summer are around noon (this varies a lot! Find a tide table first!). If you head to the rocky shore at low-low tide, **BEWARE** of the swift rise at tide turnaround. In as little as 15 minutes, the path you took to get to a pool may be flooded! Stay aware of your surroundings, and never turn your back on the ocean! If you have access to docks that sit low and float on the water, bring a flashlight and go at night! Some fishing stores even sell squid lights that you can submerge and that attract all kinds of nighttime wildlife! Often, you'll find more strange types of animals at night than during the day!

GO TIDE POOLING
OR PIER PEERING!

TIDE POOL RULES

• Never turn your back on the ocean! Waves and tides can be unpredictable, and conditions can change quickly.

• Step carefully! The rocks are covered with living animals. Do your best not to crush them, and watch your footing. Algae can be slippery, and falling onto barnacles is very painful.

• Touch animals gently! Do not pry sea stars, mussels, or snails from rocks as this can injure them. To protect soft-bodied animals from the lotions and sunscreen on your hands, and to better protect your hands from rough, barnacle-covered rocks, consider wearing gardening gloves.

• Take pictures, not souvenirs! If you want to preserve the memory of a neat shell or a beautiful hermit crab, take a photo. Please do not collect wildlife or shells. Help to preserve these public places for wildlife and other nature enthusiasts like yourself.

• Know before you go! Look up tide tables, and always be aware of the changing tides. Remember, never turn your back on the ocean!

SESSILE ANIMALS (ANIMALS THAT STAY IN ONE PLACE)

Acorn Barnacles

Giant Acorn Barnacles

Gooseneck Barnacles

Blue Mussels

Aggregating Anemones

Giant Green Anemones

Sea Squirts

MOTILE ANIMALS (ANIMALS THAT CAN MOVE)

Porcelain Crabs

Purple Shore Crabs

Green Sea Urchins

Ochre Sea Stars

GO TIDE POOLING
OR PIER PEERING!

MOTILE ANIMALS (*CONTINUED*)

Opalescent
Nudibranchs

Kelp Isopods

Black Turban
Snails

Dogwinkles

Periwinkles

Chitons

CAUTION

Large jellies
and jellies with
any yellow or
orange hues have
dangerous stinging
tentacles. Do not
touch and keep
your distance.

INSECTS & INVERTEBRATES CROSSWORD

ACROSS

2. Ochre Sea Stars, Purple Shore Crabs, and chitons are all examples of _____ **intertidal** animals

5. Metallic _____ Wasps aren't bees

7. The Opalescent _____ is a type of beautiful, feathery sea slug

9. A common garden resident with more legs than you can count!

DOWN

1. A common, fuzzy caterpillar that grows up into a Spotted Tussock Moth

3. The scientific name for fuzzy bumblebees

4. A type of intertidal snail that has nothing to do with man's best friend

6. An important pollinator, introduced from Europe as insect livestock

8. Mussels, barnacles, and sea squirts are all examples of _____ intertidal animals

Answers on page 141!

START LOOKING AT MUSHROOMS & FUNGI

Mushrooms are a common sight throughout the damp coniferous forests of the Pacific Northwest. Most fungi, like the cap mushrooms you can buy in the grocery store, are **decomposers** that dissolve decaying material around them and absorb it using an ultra-fine web of root-like structures called a **mycelium**. Most plants have an intimate and beneficial, or **mutualistic**, relationship with fungi, where they trade nutrients to the fungus in exchange for access to its impressive mycelium. This allows the plants to absorb minerals and water from the soil more efficiently and even allows them to send messages to nearby plants! This enormous underground mycelium network makes up the bulk of an individual fungus's body. That mushroom cap poking up above ground is just a small part of the whole organism. In fact, the largest organism on the planet is a honey mushroom from Malheur National Forest in northeastern Oregon. Its mycelium spans an area of approximately 1,350 soccer fields in size and is thought to be between 2,400 and 8,650 years old! And to top it all off, the honey mushroom is one of only a few fungi in the US that is **fluorescent** (glows in the dark)!

Other than gigantic glowing mushrooms, the Pacific Northwest is also home to over 4,000 species of fungi (that number doesn't include microscopic fungi like yeast or molds, and it also doesn't include lichen). With so many unique fungi, the Pacific Northwest is a popular destination for mushroom hunters and mycologists (people who study fungi). If you'd like to learn how to identify and eat wild mushrooms in your own backyard, get in touch with your local mycological society and join them for a monthly mushroom hunt! It's always best to learn from an expert before attempting to collect fungi on your own. Many species are deadly and often resemble mushrooms that look edible. Be safe and **don't eat wild mushrooms** unless they've been identified by an expert!

CAP & STEM WITH GILLS

Mushrooms with a stem and a cap, with gills underneath.

Yellow Agaric

Brilliant Waxcaps

Unidentified gill mushroom

Sulfur Tuft

Bell Omphalina

False Chanterelle

Fieldcap

Western Grisette

CAP & STEM WITH PORES

Mushrooms with a cap and a stem, with tiny holes (pores) underneath.

Rosy-ochre Suillus Bolete (upper)

Rosy-ochre Suillus Bolete (under)

Hollow-stemmed Suillus Bolete

Unidentified bolete

START LOOKING
AT MUSHROOMS & FUNGI

SHELF MUSHROOMS

Mushrooms that mostly grow out from trees, like a shelf, or a bracket; they can have either pores or gills.

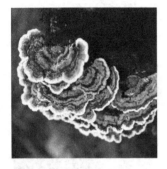

Turkey Tail

Chicken of the Woods

Giant Shelf Fungus

Cryptic Shelf Fungus

ROUND MUSHROOMS

Mushrooms that grow on the ground, in a ball or oval-like shape. Some puffballs can get as large as a soccer ball, and they're famous for "popping" and releasing a cloud of spores. But don't purposely inhale the dusty cloud they make.

Scaly Earthball

Sculpted Giant Puffball

Puffball releasing spores

Sculpted Puffball

CUP MUSHROOMS

Cup fungi are their own distinct group of mushrooms that also includes yeast, the state microbe of Oregon!

A black cup fungus

Fairy Goblet

Bird's Nest Fungus

Violet Crown Cup

SURPRISING MUSHROOMS

Mushrooms that are hard to describe because of their brain-like shapes or weird consistency.

Coral Fungus

Morel

Witches' Butter

Poor Man's Gumdrops

Cedar-Hawthorn Rust (finger stage)

Cedar-Hawthorn Rust (jelly stage)

Eyelash Cup

Stag's Horn

START LOOKING AT MUSHROOMS & FUNGI

Below and to the right are some weird things that aren't plants or animals and aren't exactly fungi. In the past, naturalists thought they might be related to fungi, but modern investigations have revealed that they're definitely not!

Slime molds, while they are called "molds," are not fungi. They're actually amoebas (single-celled organisms with special foot-like arms) that behave like a fungus. They're very diverse in wet places like temperate rainforests, and scientists are still discovering new species!

Lichens are actually a combination of two (or three!) different organisms living side-by-side in an intimate relationship called a **symbiosis**. Neither organism thrives very well on its own, but together they make some gorgeous fungus-like structures.

SLIME MOLDS

Brown Plasmodial Slime

Yellow Myxogastria Slime

Dog Vomit Plasmodial Slime

Orange Trichia Slime

LICHENS

Pincushion Xanthoria

American Rock Tripe

Wila

Brown-eyed Wolf Lichen

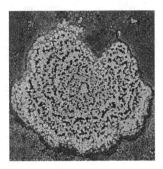
Map Lichen

Green Dog Lichen

Wolf Lichen

Warty Reindeer Lichen

TIPS FOR SPOTTING MUSHROOMS

- Look for mushrooms after a rain (they can pop up quite quickly).

- Look near the bases of dying trees or on dead logs.

- Mushrooms often seem to grow from the ground, but they might actually be growing from wood in the soil.

- Slime molds often grow under bark.

MAKE MUSHROOM SPORE PRINTS

Mushrooms reproduce via spores. Spores are too small to see individually without a microscope, but there's an easy and fun way to spot them: by making a spore print. For a number of technical reasons, spores aren't considered the same thing as a seed in a plant, but the basic idea is the same: spores help fungi reproduce. And they do that by leaving microscopic spores behind almost everywhere. Spore colors vary by species, and they can produce some neat results. To see for yourself, make a spore print.

WHAT YOU'LL NEED

• Small bowls or cups

• White paper and, if possible, some construction paper of various colors

• Different kinds of mushrooms, with caps and pores, or caps and gills; collect a variety of them, if possible

WHAT TO DO

With a knife, cut off the cap of each mushroom—or take a good section of a shelf mushroom—and place it on top of a piece of paper. (The gills or pores should be facing down onto the paper.) Place a small bowl or a cup over each mushroom. Mushroom spore colors vary a lot, so it's helpful to change up the paper color; a mushroom with light-colored spores won't show up well on white paper, for instance. Wait an hour or so, remove the bowl, and throw the mushroom in the trash. Then admire the spore print left behind!

Important Note: Have an adult handle the knife, and don't make spore prints in your kitchen or another area where food is served, or where someone could mistake the mushrooms for food. A garage is a good place to make spore prints.

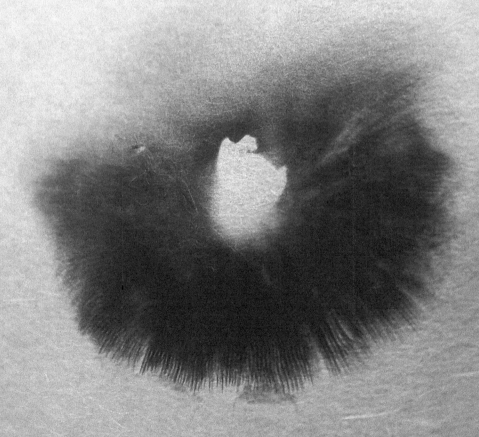

CARVE ARTIST'S CONK

Artist's Conk is a special kind of shelf mushroom that grows on dead or dying trees. At first glance, it doesn't look like much. It's pretty plain looking on the top—oval shaped and brown and white—and underneath it's just a drab white.

Artist's Conk gets its name because its white pores turn a dark brown when scratched. And the scratches then stay that way, making it a favorite of "scratch artists." This makes Artist's Conk something like nature's Etch A Sketch.

Of course, to identify Artist's Conk, you'll need an adult's help and a field guide (see page 136), but it's not too tricky to spot once you start looking.

Before you carve your Artist's Conk, you might want to practice writing down your message here. When you're writing on a mushroom, you can't use an eraser, so practicing here first can help you get it right.

_____

_____

_____

_____

_____

_____

_____

_____

_____

_____

QUICK QUIZ

The Pacific Northwest is famous for several types of fungi, two of which are honored as state symbols. What are they? **Hint:** One is related to cup fungi, but it is actually a single-celled organism!

_____

_____

Answers on page 140!

CONDUCT A BACKYARD BIO-BLITZ

A bio-blitz is an event where nature lovers—usually in a large group—try to record all of the life in a given area during a set period of time. But you don't need to be a scientist to do a bio-blitz; you can do one yourself or with your family. And you can do one wherever you are: in your backyard, on a trip, even from the window of a car or from an apartment balcony. The basic idea is simple: you want to try to identify as many lifeforms as you can within a certain amount of time.

WHAT YOU WILL NEED

• A magnifying glass

• A smartphone

• A notebook and pen for each person

• Field guides

WHAT TO DO

The simplest way to start off is in your backyard or a green space near where you live. Have an adult set a timer for 15 minutes. Start out with the easy stuff first: the grass, any weeds that you recognize (dandelions), and birds or mammals (such as chipmunks or squirrels). It's helpful to be systematic: start in one area, and look it over carefully before moving on to the next.

For each life form you find, write down what you think it is and where you found it. Take a picture, or draw it if you don't know what it is and want to look it up. See how many different kinds of animals and plants you can find, and record them on the form to the right!

Bonus: If you can look it up, try to find the scientific name for what you found. Scientific names exist to make it easier for scientists to talk to each other clearly. For example, there are three main different kinds of bears in North America: American Black Bears, Brown Bears, and Polar Bears. So the word *bear* isn't very specific. And for many creatures, including insects, there simply aren't any common names. A scientific name is a special name that has two parts: a **genus name,** which is like a last name and is shared with other similar animals, and a **species name**, which is like a first name. Together, that name is unique for that animal. For example, only one plant has the name *Taraxacum officinale*: the Common Dandelion, and scientists all over the world can refer to it, even if they don't speak the same language!

Note: If you're doing this from a car window on a long drive, you obviously won't be able to take photos. However, you can still note the birds, trees, roadside plants and such that you see, and any deer, foxes, Coyotes, or other critters along the way.

WHAT IS IT?	LOCATION	SCIENTIFIC NAME
Plants		
Dandelion	By the swing set	*Taraxacum officinale*
Douglas-fir cone	In the front yard	*Pseudotsuga menziesii*
Birds		
American Robin	On the lawn	*Turdus migratorius*
Mammals		
Gray Squirrel		
Insects		
Unidentified but Cool		

CONTRIBUTE TO A COMMUNITY SCIENCE PROJECT

Community science projects are opportunities for regular people to contribute and participate in a big science experiment. Some of the most famous, oldest community science projects include the Christmas Bird Count, which started in the year 1900, and SETI@home, which allows regular people to assist in analyzing radio waves in the search for extraterrestrial intelligence. If you'd like to find and participate in a community science project, visit SciStarter.org and get your parents help to sign up for one that interests you. We've included our favorites below.

iNATURALIST

iNaturalist is a smartphone app that allows people to identify and submit their photos of plants and animals. Any photo of something in nature can become a scientific data point if you include the date and location where you found it! The creators of iNaturalist knew that with so many mobile devices and cameras out in the world today, there was an opportunity to learn a lot about the natural world!

HOW TO PARTICIPATE

If your parents have a smartphone, or you have one, ask if it's OK to download iNaturalist. Once you sign up (you have to be 13 years old to have your own account), all you have to do is take a photo of an animal, plant, or mushroom. You then create an observation, add the photo, and click on the "What Did You See?" button. The app will run the photo through a computer program that will attempt to identify it; the program isn't perfect, but it often helps you narrow down what you found.

Then, if you share the observation and location online, other observers (including experts) can help confirm your identification (or propose a new one). Once an observation has two identifications that are the same, it's considered "research grade," and it can be used by scientists! In particular, scientists studying animals and plants living in and around cities are using iNaturalist photos to learn more about how humans and wildlife are adapting to coexist. And photos taken in remote areas while on hunting or backpacking trips provide data for regions that the biologists might not be able to visit. Even something as simple as taking pictures of the moths visiting your porch lights can lead to invaluable scientific discoveries! Remember, any photo can become a scientific data point as long as it has a date and location!

Note: If you're worried about posting your location, there's an option to click "obscured" under geolocation. This prevents people from seeing exactly where you made your observation and instead only gives a large range instead.

eBIRD

Like iNaturalist, eBird uses observations from regular people to make scientific discoveries! If you're a bird nerd, like I am, eBird is a great way to tell scientists where and when you've seen a certain bird. Unlike iNaturalist, you don't need a photo to complete your submission. Instead, scientists rely on you to know what bird species you're observing. Fortunately, their webpage provides a lot of helpful information if you need assistance identifying a bird in your backyard.

CONTRIBUTE TO A COMMUNITY SCIENCE PROJECT

HOW TO PARTICIPATE

Just like iNaturalist, eBird has a mobile app that you can download and use to submit your observations in the field. Remember to always ask your parents before downloading new applications. If you don't have a smartphone, eBird also allows users to submit observations on their webpage. The project is run by the Cornell Lab of Ornithology that also provides some of North America's best information on birds (they also have a free website called AllAboutBirds).

You'll need to create an account to submit your observations. Get your parents help with this. Then, next time you're on a walk or just out in your backyard, write down which and how many birds you see. Don't forget to write down where and when you saw them! Then, follow the instructions on eBird.org or on the app to complete the submission. You can even view what others have seen in your area using the "Explore" button.

Keep track of your community science discoveries here by making a "life list" of the plants, animals, and fungi you've spotted.

_____

_____

_____

_____

_____

_____

_____

_____

_____

_____

_____

_____

_____

_____

_____

_____

NATURE BINGO

Circle the nature you see, and see who gets a bingo first!

NATURE

BINGO

DANDELION	BEE	MAMMAL	PINE NEEDLE	GRASS
CONIFEROUS TREE	ROCK	MOSS	GRASSHOPPER	CLOUD
SPIDER	ANT	FREE THE SKY SPACE	BEETLE	DECIDUOUS TREE
THE MOON	WORM	BIRD	LOG	STAR (THE SUN COUNTS!)
MUSHROOM	MAPLE LEAF	PINE CONE	BUTTERFLY	FROG

NATURE

BINGO

MOSS	BEE	MAMMAL	WORM	DECIDUOUS TREE
ANT	BIRD	DANDELION	CONIFEROUS TREE	SPIDER
ROCK	GRASSHOPPER	FREE THE SKY SPACE	PINE CONE	BEETLE
THE MOON	PINE NEEDLE	GRASS	STAR (THE SUN COUNTS!)	FROG
MAPLE LEAF	LOG	MUSHROOM	CLOUD	BUTTERFLY

RECORD YOUR ACTIVITIES, DISCOVERIES & FINDS HERE

Did you find a neat feather, leaf, rock, or other natural object? Record your discovery by writing down your observations below and making a sketch to the right!

Date _____

Location _____

Weather & Temperature_____

Observations _____

_____

_____

_____

_____

_____

_____

_____

_____

_____

_____

_____

RECORD YOUR ACTIVITIES, DISCOVERIES & FINDS HERE

Did you find a neat feather, leaf, rock, or other natural object? Record your discovery by writing down your observations below and making a sketch to the right!

Date _____

Location _____

Weather & Temperature_____

Observations _____

_____

_____

_____

_____

_____

_____

_____

_____

_____

_____

_____

0 inch 1 2 3 4 5 6 7 8 9 10

RECORD YOUR ACTIVITIES, DISCOVERIES & FINDS HERE

Did you find a neat feather, leaf, rock, or other natural object? Record your discovery by writing down your observations below and making a sketch to the right!

Date _____

Location _____

Weather & Temperature_____

Observations _____

_____

_____

_____

_____

_____

_____

_____

_____

_____

_____

RECORD YOUR ACTIVITIES, DISCOVERIES & FINDS HERE

Did you find a neat feather, leaf, rock, or other natural object? Record your discovery by writing down your observations below and making a sketch to the right!

Date _____

Location _____

Weather & Temperature_____

Observations _____

_____

_____

_____

_____

_____

_____

_____

_____

_____

_____

0 inch 1 2 3 4 5 6 7 8 9 10

RECOMMENDED READING

Daniels, Jaret C. *Backyard bugs: An Identification Guide to Common Insects, Spiders, and More.* Cambridge, Minnesota: Adventure Publications, 2017.

Eisner, Thomas. *For Love of Insects.* Cambridge, Mass: Belknap Press of Harvard University Press, 2003.

Lynch, Dan R. *Fossils for Kids: An Introduction to Paleontology.* Cambridge, Minnesota: Adventure Publications, 2020.

Lynch, Dan R. *Rock Collecting for Kids: An Introduction to Geology.* Cambridge, Minnesota: Adventure Publications, 2018.

ADVANCED GUIDES TO EXPAND YOUR KNOWLEDGE

Bradley, Richard A. *Common Spiders of North America.* University of California Press, 2012.

Elbroch, Mark, and Casey McFarland. *Mammal Tracks & Sign: A Guide to North American Species.* 2nd ed. Rowman & Littlefield, 2019.

Harbo, Rick M. *Whelks to Whales: Coastal Marine Life of the Pacific Northwest.* Harbour Publishing Company, 1999.

Hitchcock, C. Leo, and Arthur Cronquist. *Flora of the Pacific Northwest: An illllustrated Manual.* 2nd ed. University of Washington Press, 2018.

McCune, Bruce, and Linda Geiser. *Macrolichens of the Pacific Northwest.* 2nd ed. Oregon State University Press, 2009.

Peterson, Merrill A. *Pacific Northwest Insects.* Seattle, Washington: Seattle Audubon Society, 2018.

Trudell, Steve, and Joe Ammirati. *Mushrooms of the Pacific Northwest.* Timber Press, 2009.

GLOSSARY

Biome A community of animals and plants that live in a specific kind of climate and environment.

Chalcedony A banded form of quartz that is popular as a collectible.

Chemical element One of the 92 naturally occurring chemicals, such as oxygen, carbon, etc., that make up all matter on Earth.

Commodities Farm products that are sold worldwide.

Conifer A tree that produces seeds by cones; most conifers, but not all, are evergreen.

Decomposer An organism that breaks down (decomposes) the dead tissues of other organisms.

Dormant A sleep-like state when a plant or animal is not active.

Endemic An organism that is unique to a certain area (usually fairly small) and found nowhere else on Earth.

Eroded Material, especially rock or soil, that has worn away due to water and wind over time.

Equator The midpoint on the earth's surface between the North and South Poles; the days and nights are always equal in length, and the latitude measurement is 0.

Evergreen A tree that doesn't lose its leaves and stays green all winter.

Extinct When a species no longer exists on Earth.

Fluorescent A material that glows, or emits light, when it absorbs energy like light (especially ultraviolet light).

Fossil A once-living organism whose dead body has been replaced with rock (mineralized) over time.

GLOSSARY

Genus name Because there are so many different plants and animals and other lifeforms, scientists give every organism one name, usually derived from Latin/Greek. This scientific name has two parts: a genus, which is like an organism's last name, and which it shares with others, and its species name, which is like its first name.

So if you want to talk to a scientist about the American Robin, *Turdus migratorius* is the name that scientists would recognize all around the world. (And really, that's its real scientific name).

Geode A round rock that contains an empty space inside it often with crystals inside; when broken in half, geodes are popular collectibles.

Glaciers Huge rivers of ice that once covered much of the country creating much of the topography we see (or don't!) today.

Intertidal The part of the beach that's underwater during high tide but exposed during low tide.

Introduced An animal or plant that was brought to an area (example: cows in the US).

Living Fossil An organism that appears remarkably similar to its fossilized, prehistoric ancestors.

Mineral A chemical combination of two or more elements; individual elements (like copper and gold) are considered minerals as well.

Mohs Hardness Scale The relative scale of mineral hardness, from the softest, talc (1), to the hardest, diamond (10).

Mutualistic A relationship between two organisms where each one gets something of value/or benefit.

Mycelium The underground, root-like network of tiny, thread-like tissues that makes up most of a fungus's body.

Native An animal, plant or organism found naturally in an area.

Non-native An animal, plant, or organism not naturally found in an area; **note:** not all non-native animals are invasive.

Orion (constellation) A group of stars named for a hunter in ancient Greek mythology.

Parasite An animal or organism that feeds on or otherwise depends on another animal, plant or organism.

Phenology The study of the seasons and other natural cycles over time.

Predators Animals that eat other animals.

Rock A combination of two or more minerals.

Species name See genus.

Symbiosis When two different organisms interact; sometimes, this interaction is beneficial for both (known as mutualism). At other times, one organism thrives at the expense of another (known as parasitism).

Temperate An environment where there are long periods (summer!) where the weather is warm.

Toxic Poisonous

Translucent Something (often a mineral) that allows light to pass through it.

QUICK QUIZ ANSWERS

Page 5: Boise, Idaho; Salem, Oregon; Olympia, Washington

Page 11: B. Subalpine Fir

Page 17: B. Native and restricted to a certain area

Page 24: Olympic Marmot, Idaho Giant Salamander

Page 43: Huckleberries and Chanterelles are not included because they can't be grown, they can only be harvested from the wild

Page 49: Opal and obsidian

Page 77: Washington endemic mammal: Olympic Marmot
Washington marine mammal: Orca
Washington fossil: Columbian Mammoth
Oregon animal: Beaver
Idaho fossil: Hagerman Horse
Idaho horse: Appaloosa

Page 79: 1. Two; 2. Animals with webbed toes live near water. The Beaver has webbed toes.

Page 93: Idaho: Monarch Butterfly (Lepidoptera)
Oregon: Oregon Swallowtail (Lepidoptera)
Washington: Green Darner (Odonata)

Page 98: 1. Flower Scarab; 2. Hoverfly; 3. Bumblebee

Page 119: Oregon state mushroom: Pacific Golden Chanterelle
Oregon state microbe: Brewer's Yeast

CROSSWORD ANSWERS

Geology & Gemstones, page 55:

Insects & Invertebrates, page 109:

ABOUT THE AUTHOR

Dr. Robert Niese is a lifelong nature nut and has been collecting and identifying plants, animals, fungi, rocks, and fossils ever since he was a child exploring California's diverse habitats. As an undergraduate at the University of Puget Sound in Tacoma, Washington, his hobbies became invaluable skills when he was hired by the Slater Museum of Natural History to write and implement science curricula for hundreds of elementary school classrooms throughout western Washington. In 2013, Robert took his enthusiasm and expertise for Pacific Northwest flora and fauna to Montana where he received his Ph.D. in comparative vertebrate anatomy and, in his free time, wrote nature journal entries for his blog, Northwest Naturalist, which has thousands of followers. Today, Robert continues to teach college students about mammals, plants, birds, and bones throughout the Pacific Northwest.

ACKNOWLEDGMENTS

To all the naturalists who came before me, to those who took the time to connect me to nature, and to those who never stopped encouraging my curiosity.

DEDICATION

For curious kids and adults everywhere.

PHOTO CREDITS

All photos are copyright of their respective photographers.

Front and back cover images used under license from Shutterstock. Front cover and title page: **Birdiegal:** bird; **Bob Pelletier:** butterfly; **next143:** binoculars; **Steve Mann:** ruler; **tab62:** flowers; **Vitaly Korovin:** magnifying glass; **Vitaly Zorkin:** pencil

Back cover: **Svetlana Foote:** Inchworm

All images copyright by Robert Niese unless otherwise noted:

Justin Bastow: 25 (Petrified Wood); **Paul Cryan, U.S. Geological Survey:** 76 (Spotted Bat); **Idaho Fish and Game Diane Evans-Mack:** 77 (right); **Ryan Hagerty, USFWS:** 22 (left), 77 (middle); **Jeff Knight, Nevada Department of Agriculture State Entomologist:** 17 (bottom); **Matt Lavin:** 11 (C); **Library of Congress:** 22 (middle); **Steve Lonhart (SIMoN/MBNMS):** 108 (Black Turban Snails); **Brett Ortler:** 52 (both), 57 (bottom), 64, 65, 69 (bottom), 74, 117 (both), 118 (all); **Duncan Pay/© GIA:** 26 (Oregon Sunstone); **Martin Raphael, U.S. Forest Service:** 59 (Marbled Murrelet); **M.O. Stevens:** 46 (bottom); **Montana Natural Heritage Program/Eric Dallalio and Bryce Maxell:** 27 (Idaho Giant Salamander); **MPalmquist:** 27 (Western White Pine); **National Park Service:** 59 (Black Oystercatcher, Red-breasted Sapsucker, Auklet, Grouse, Varied Thrush), 60 (Dusky Grouse); **National Park Service, J. Preston:** 5 (Chestnut-backed Chickadee); **National Park Service, Jacob W. Frank:** 36 (Western Tanager), 61 (Lazuli Bunting); **National Park Service, Jay Fleming:** 27 (Cutthroat Trout); **Jim Nieland, USFS:** 18 (Mt. St. Helens 1979); **Robert Niese (c) Slater Museum of Natural History:** 15 (all); **Alejandro Santilana, Insects Unlocked, University of Texas at Austin:** 91 (Walking Stick); **ALAN SCHMIERER:** 26 (Oregon Swallowtail); **Stephan Schulz:** 18 (Mt. St. Helens 2012); **U.S. Library of Congress:** 22 (right); **Washington Geological Survey:** 21 (top); and **Fallon Venable:** 128-135 (Background Illustrations).

Images used under license from Shutterstock: **Adrian_am13:** 113 (Violet Crown Cup); **Agami Photo Agency:** 60 (Red-naped Sapsucker); **Agnieszka Bacal:** 41 (Bighorn Sheep), 61 (Greater Sage Grouse); **Alexander62:** 113 (Eyelash Cup); **Amelia Marti:** 113 (Cedar-Hawthorn Rust); **Andriy Kananovych:** 48 (bottom), 50 (all), 51 (all); **aniana:** 13 (top right); **Arno van Dulmen:** 92 (Orb Weaver); **Bermek:** 12; **Bob Pool:** 10 (top), 76 (River Otter), 92 (Pill Bug); **Breck P. Kent:** 26 (Dawn Redwood); **brizmaker:** 73; **Caleb Jones Photo:** 60 (Canada Jay); **CEW:** 63; **Chad Hutchinson:** 27 (Potato); **Cheryl Thomas:** 27 (Monarch Butterfly); **christopher babcock:** 108 (bottom); **Cynthia Kidwell:** 37 (Pronghorn and calf); **Dafinchi:** 48 (top); **Dan Baillie:** 58 (European Starling); **Daniel Luk:** 41 (Bald Eagles); **Danita Delimont:** 16 (bottom), 34 (bottom); **DarrenWagner:** 40 (Chum Salmon); **David McMillan:** 58 (Northern Flicker); **Dawn Umstot:** 21 (bottom); **Denis Pogostin:** 43 (left); **Dennis W Donohue:** 61 (Say's Phoebe); **Elenarts:** 25 (Columbian Mammoth); **Elizabeth A.Cummings:** 17 (top); **Eric Eric:** 25 (apple); **Ferenc Speder:** 53 (bottom); **galitsin:** 93 (Earthworm); **Gerald A. DeBoer:** 61 (Prairie Falcon); **giedre vaitekune:** 43 (right); **Gorka Liberal:** 124; **gregg williams:** 25 (Willow Goldfinch); **Ibe van Oort:** 47 (top); **Intellson:** 129, 131, 133 & 135 (Ruler); **Ira Shpiller:** 43 (middle); **Ja Het:** 49 (top); **Jacob Boomsma:** 47 (bottom); **Jason Burnett:** 41 (Short-eared Owl); **jeanm:** 123; **Jennifer Bosvert:** 99 (Metallic Green Bee); **Jillian Cain Photography:** 72 (bottom); **Jody Ann:** 26 (American Beaver); **Jonathan Lingel:** 25 (Sweet Onion); **Jordan Feeg:** 58 (American Robin); **Joseph Sohm:** 7 (top left); **Jovana Kuzmanovic:** 92 (Centipede); **Katyna Kon:** 26 (Brewer's Yeast); **Kevin Cass:** 26 (Chinook Salmon); **Kirk Geisler:** 61 (Sage Thrasher); **Kristi Blokhin:** 72 (top); **Kyle J Jensen:** 27 (Huckleberry); **Lecsposure:** 57 (top); **Lenxoxo:** 13 (bottom right); **Lindaimke:** 58 (Red-tailed Hawk); **Losonsky:** 59 (Steller's Jay); **Mike Gostomski:** 7 (bottom right); **Minakryn Ruslan:** 46 (middle); **Mindful Photography:** 79 (bottom); **Mircea Costina:** 58 (American Crow), 60 (Pine Grosbeak); **MTKhaled mahmud:** 61 (Rough-legged Hawk); **My Generations Art:** 60 (Mountain Chickadee); **MyImages - Micha:** 13 (top left); **Nadzeya Leanovich:** 79 (top); **Natalya Rozhkova:** 78; **Nikki Yancey:** 11 (B), 38 (Yellow Pond Lily); **Orest lyzhechka:** 113 (Stag's Horn); **Patrick Ziegler:** 61 (Yellow-headed Blackbird); **Paul Reeves Photography:** 98 (1); **Paul Roedding:** 34 (middle); **Phil64:** 27 (Star Garnet), 48 (middle); **poylock19:** 67; **punkbirdr:** 59 (Hermit Warbler); **Rachel Zoller-Box:** 26 (Pacific Golden Chanterelle), 114 (Orange Trichia Slime); **Randy Bjorklund:** 76 (Sagebrush Vole), 77 (left), 107 (Purple Shore Crab); **rck_953:** 61 (Black-

Photo Credits *(continued)*

chinned Hummingbird); **RENA MICHAEL:** 112 (Sculpted Puffball); **Robert Paulus:** 62 (Evening Grosbeak); **Rose Ludwig:** 86 (Paper Wasp); **Sara Winter:** 14; **Sean Lema:** 25 (Steelhead Trout); **Sophia Cole:** 36 (Ponderosa Pine Pollen); **Stefan Schug:** 13 (bottom left); **Stephanie Kenner:** 105; **Sundry Photography:** 122; **Suzana Lutterman:** 95 (bottom); **teekaygee:** 25 (Pacific Chorus Frog); **Thorsten Spoerlein:** 58 (Mallard); **Tom Reichner:** 58 (Mourning Dove), 60 (Harlequin Duck & Lewis's Woodpecker), 66; Tomsickova Tatyana: 54; **Tory Kallman:** 25 (Orca); **William Cushman:** 25 (Olympic Marmot); **William T Smith:** 40 (Sandhill Crane); **Wirestock Creators:** 46 (top); **Wojciech Lepczynski:** 95 (top); **YegoroV:** 104; and **Zuzule:** 27 (Appaloosa).

Map Citations:

Biomes of the PNW (pg 8-9) - Data source: USGS, Esri

Volcanoes (pg 19) - Map after Christiansen and Others (2007) and Barry and Others (2013).

Ice Age Floods (pg 20) - Map after Waitt (2016).

Tribes (pg 23) - Data Source: US Census Bureau

NATURE JOURNALS FOR KIDS
— from —
ADVENTURE PUBLICATIONS

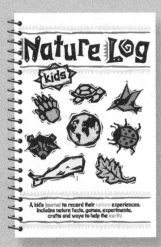
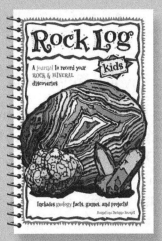
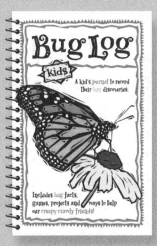

- Guided journaling pages
- Fascinating information
- Fun activities for the family
- Photo and art pages

SAFETY NOTE

Nature is wonderful and amazing, and it's certainly nothing to be afraid of, especially if you use common sense and take precautions.

Many of these places bring us into close contact with wildlife and plants, some of which can be harmful to unwary young naturalists. We encourage you to wear long pants and long-sleeve shirts whenever you are exploring wild spaces to protect against stinging or biting insects, ticks, poisonous plants, and sunburn. Remember, venomous animals like spiders, bees, wasps, ants, sea jellies, and scorpions will not harm you if you keep your distance and don't harm them. Our most dangerous animals in the Pacific Northwest are rattlesnakes, deer, and Black Bears. Do not approach these animals even if they appear tame.

Whenever you go out into nature, it's good to be prepared for its hazards. Bring sunscreen, plenty of water, and an EpiPen if you have severe allergies (to bees, for example), and dress for the weather. Most importantly, be aware of your surroundings (watch the tides, don't stray from the trails, etc.), and keep your distance from wild animals. Remember: You are responsible for your safety!

An especially important note: Don't use this book to help you identify which wild plants, berries, fruits, or mushrooms are safe to eat. Please leave the berries, fruits, and mushrooms you find for the birds, critters, and the bugs. Instead, get your snacks from the fridge!

Edited by Brett Ortler

Cover and book design by Fallon Venable

Backyard Nature and Science Workbook: Pacific Northwest Fun Activities and Experiments That Get Kids Outdoors
Copyright © 2021 by Dr. Robert Niese
Published by Adventure Publications
An imprint of AdventureKEEN
310 Garfield Street South
Cambridge, Minnesota 55008
(800) 678-7006
www.adventurepublications.net
All rights reserved
Printed in the United States of America
ISBN: 978-1-64755-171-1

CPSIA information can be obtained
at www.ICGtesting.com
Printed in the USA
JSHW042209200521
14888JS00007B/13